The Tale of Star-Oddi's Dream

Original Text, Translations, and Word Lists

Translated by
Matthew Leigh Embleton

Copyright ©2025 Matthew Leigh Embleton. All rights reserved.

The Tale of Star-Oddi's Dream

The Tale of Star-Oddi's Dream (*Old Norse*) 4
Word List *(Old Norse to English)*..35
Word List *(English to Old Norse)* 53
The Tale of Star-Oddi's Dream (*Old Icelandic*) 68
Word List *(Old Icelandic to English)*...99
Word List *(English to Old Icelandic)*...117
A Word Comparison of Old Norse and Old Icelandic Words 132

Cover: Old Norse text over an outline of Iceland. Author's design.

The original Old Norse and Old Icelandic texts are in the public domain.
These translations ©2022 Matthew Leigh Embleton
©2025 Matthew Leigh Embleton (This Edition)

Acknowledgments

I have long been fascinated by languages and history, and I am very grateful to the special people in my life who have supported and encouraged me in my work. Thank you for believing in me. You know who you are.

Introduction

Old Norse is a North Germanic language spoken by inhabitants of Scandinavia from about the 7th to the 15th centuries. Old Icelandic is a variety of Old West Norse that emerged during the Norse settlement of Iceland in the second half of the 9th century. The rich tradition of Icelandic literature survived by oral tradition over several centuries before being written down in the 13th Century. The Tale of Star-Oddi's Dream (*Stjörnu-Odda draumr*) is one of the many Tales of Icelanders or *Íslendingaþættir*. The word '*þáttr*' (plural: '*þættir*') translates as a strand of rope or a yarn, comparable to the word 'yarn' in English sometimes used to refer to a story.

This book contains:
- The Tale of Star-Oddi's Dream (*Stjörnu-Odda draumr*) (Old Norse Version)
- An Old Norse to English Word List
- An English to Old Norse Word List
- The Tale of Star-Oddi's Dream (*Stjörnu-Odda draumr*) (Old Icelandic Version)
- An Old Icelandic to English Word List
- An English to Old Icelandic Word List
- A Word Comparison of Old Norse and Old Icelandic words

The texts are presented in their original form, with a literal word-for-word line-by-line translation, and a Modern English translation, all side-by-side. In this way, it is possible to see and feel how the worked and how it has evolved. This book is designed to be of use and interest to anyone with a passion for the Old Norse or Old Icelandic language, Norse history, or languages and history in general.

The Tale of Star-Oddi's Dream (*Old Norse*)

Old Norse	Literal	English
1	**1**	**1**
Þórðr hét maðr, er bjó í Múla norðr í Reykjardal.	Thord was-named a-man, who lived at Muli in-the-north in Reykjardal.	There was a man named Thord who lived at Muli in the north, in Reykjardal.
Þar var á vist með honum sá maðr, er Oddi hét ok var Helgason.	There was in hospitality with him so a-man, who Oddi named and was Son-of-Helgi.	There was a man living with him named Oddi who was the son of Helgi.
Hann var kallaðr Stjörnu-Oddi.	He was called Star-Oddi.	He was called Star-Oddi.
Hann var rímkænn maðr, svá at engi maðr var hans maki honum samtíða á öllu Íslandi, ok at mörgu var hann annars vitr.	He was calendar-computation-wise a-man, so that no man was his match him contemporary in all Iceland, and that many was he otherwise wise.	He was skilled in the art of calendar computation, such that no man in all of Iceland was a match for him, and he was also wise in many other things.
Ekki var hann skáld né kvæðinn.	Not was he poet nor poetry.	He was not a poet, nor did he know much poetry.
Þess er ok einkum getit um hans ráð, at þat höfðu menn fyrir satt, at hann lygi aldri, ef hann vissi satt at segja, ok at öllu var hann ráðvandr kallaðr ok tryggðarmaðr inn mesti.	This was also particularly told about his statements, that it had people before the-truth, that he lied never, if he knew the-truth to say, and that all was he honest called and faithful-man the most.	It was also particularly said about him of his statements that people held them to be the truth, that he never lied if he knew the truth to tell, and that he was the most honest and faithful man.
Félítill var hann ok ekki mikill verkmaðr.	Fee-little was he and not much working-man.	He was poor and not an especially good worker.
Frá því er at segja, at um þenna mann, Odda, gerðist undarligr atburðr.	From therefore is to say, that about this man, Oddi, happened extraordinary events.	The story goes that extraordinary events happened to this man Oddi.
Hann fór heiman út til Flateyjar, er Þórðr, húsbóndi hans, sendi hann þessa ferð á vit fiska, ok er eigi annars getit en þeim fórst vel til eyjarinnar.	He travelled home out-from to Flatey, when Thord, housemaster his, sent him this journey to to fishing, and was not anything-else told-of but they travelled well to the-island.	He travelled out from his home to Flatey when his housemaster Thord sent him on a journey to go fishing, and nothing else is told except that the journey to the island went well.
Þar var hann í góðum beina.	There was he in good assistance.	He was well looked after there.

The Tale of Star-Oddi's Dream (Old Norse)

Old Norse	Literal	English
Ekki er frá því sagt, hverr þar bjó.	Not was from therefore said, who there lived.	It was not said who lived there.
En frá því er at segja, at um kveldit, er menn fóru í rekkju, var vel búit um Odda ok hægliga,	Then from therefore was it said, that about evening, were people going to bed, was well preparations about Oddi and comfortable,	Then from there it was said that about one evening people were going to bed, as preparations were made to make Oddi comfortable.
en við þat, er Oddi var farmóðr ok veittr hógligr umbúnaðr, þá sofnar hann brátt, ok dreymði hann þegar, at hann þóttist staddr vera heima í Múla, ok svá þótti honum sem þar væri kominn maðr til gistingar, ok þótti honum sem menn færi í rekkju um kveldit.	and with that, was Oddi was travel-weary and given comfortably soft-bed-prepared, then slept he soon, and dreamed he straightaway, that he though stood was home in Muli, and so seemed to-him that there was come a-man to guest, and thought he as people went to bed about evening.	And with Oddi being travel-weary, he was given a comfortable and soft bed that had been prepared for him, and he soon fell asleep and dreamed straightaway that he stood at home in Muli, and it seemed to him that a man had come as a guest, and that people were going to bed in the evening.
Þótti honum gestrinn vera beðinn skemmtanar, en hann tók til ok sagði sögu ok hóf á þessa leið:	Seemed to-him the-guest was asking entertainment, and he took to of the-saga telling and began in this way:	It seemed to him that the guest had asked for some entertainment, and he took to telling a saga, which began in this way.

2 | # 2 | # 2

Old Norse	Literal	English
Hróðbjartr hefir konungr heitit.	Hrodbjart had king dominion.	Hrodbart had the rule of a king.
Hann réð austr fyrir Gautlandi.	He ruled east for Götaland.	He ruled over east Götaland.
Hann var kvángaðr maðr.	He was married man.	He was a married man.
Hildiguðr hét kona hans.	Hildigunn named wife his.	His wife was named Hildigunn.
Þau áttu sér einn son barna, er Geirviðr er nefndr.	They had themselves only son child, was Geirvid was named.	They had an only child whose was named Geirvid.
Hann var snemma vænn ok vitmikill ok at öllum hlutum mannaðr um fram sína jafnaldra, en barn var hann at aldri, er sagan gerðist.	He was soon handsome and knowing-much and in all things brought-up about from his equal-age, but child was he of age, when the-saga begins.	He grew up to be handsome and wise in all things more than those his age, but he was a child when the saga begins.

The Tale of Star-Oddi's Dream (Old Norse)

Old Norse	Literal	English
Frá því er at segja, at konungrinn Hróðbjartr hafði settan til landstjórnar yfir þriðjung ríkis síns jarl þann, er Hjörvarðr hét.	From therefore is to say, that this-king Hrodbjart had appointed to governing over a-third-of kingdom his earl then, was Hjorvard named.	From there is to say that this King Hrodbjart had appointed an earl to govern over a third of the kingdom who was named Hjorvard.
Hann var ok kvángaðr, ok hét kona hans Hjörguðr,	He was also married, and named wife his Hjorgunn,	He was also married and his wife was named Hjorgunn.
Þau áttu eina dóttur barna.	They had only daughter child.	They had a daughter who was an only child.
Sú hét Hléguðr.	So named Hlegunn.	She was named Hlegunn.
Frá henni er svá sagt, at hon var ólát í æsku sinni, ok var ávallt því ódælli sem hon var eldri.	From her is so said, that she was un-courteous in youth hers, and was always therefore un-pleasant as she was older.	It is said of her that she was discourteous in her youth and got more unpleasant as she got older.
Þat var ok sagt, at hon vildi ekki kvennasið fága í sínu athæfi.	It was also said, that she willed not woman's-customs cultivate in her behaviour.	It was also said that she did not wish to cultivate womanly traditions in her behaviour.
Þat var hennar venja jafnan, at hon gekk í herklæðum ok með vápnum, ok ef hana skildi á við menn, þá veitti hon þeim annathvárt áverka stóra eða líflát, þegar henni líkaði eigi.	It was her way always, that she went in war-clothes and with weapons, and if she should then against people, then gave her them either-way injury great or life-less, as-soon-as she liked not.	It was always her way that she went about in armour with weapons, and if people went against her in any way she gave them either a great injury or death as soon as she did not like them.
En við þenna hennar ójafnað þá þótti Hjörvarði jarli, föður hennar, eigi mega við sæma hennar vandræði ok sagði henni þá ljósliga, at hann mundi eigi þann veg lengr láta fram fara, ok kvað henni eigi hlýða mundu, nema um batnaði nökkurs háttar,	Then with this her unequal then thought Hjorvard the-earl, father hers, not may with the-same her difficulty and told her then lightly, that he may not then way longer let from go, and said she not obey would, except about bettering somewhat kind,	Then with this overbearing behaviour, her father earl Hjorvard felt that he may not tolerate her disruptions any more, and told her plainly that it could not go on any longer, and that she should do somewhat better,
"eða elligar far í brott sem skjótast ór minni hirð",	"or otherwise travel to away as soonest from my court",	or otherwise leave my court as soon as possible.

The Tale of Star-Oddi's Dream (Old Norse)

Old Norse	Literal	English
En þegar Hléguðr jarlsdóttir verðr þessa áheyrsla af feðr sínum, at hann vildi hana láta í burt fara af sinni hirð, þá svarar hon því máli svá, at hon kvað sik þar ekki dvelja, ok beiddi hon þá föður sinn, at hann skyldi fá henni langskip þrjú, alskipuð bæði at mönnum ok herklæðum, ok búa at öllu sem bezt með góðum liðskosti, svá at henni þætti vel skipuð,	Then as-soon-as Hlegunn the-earl's-daughter became of-this to-hear of father hers, that he willed her leave to away travel from his court, then answered she therefore saying so, that she spoke herself there not dwell, and asked she then father hers, that he should give her longships three, fully-prepared both in men and war-clothes, and prepare that all as best with good provisions, so that she seemed well prepared,	Then as soon as the earl's daughter Hlegunn came to hear of her father, that he wished her to travel away from his court, then she answered therefore declaring, that she did not wish to stay there and asked her father to give her three longships fully prepared with men and armour, and prepared with the best provisions so that she was well prepared.
ok ef svá væri gert sem hon beiddi hér um þetta mál, þá talði hon sér mundu vel líka, þótt hon færi í braut við svá búit.	and if so would-be done as she asked she about that matter, then said she herself would well like, thought she travel to away with so prepared.	And if it would be done as she asked in this matter then she said she would like to travel away as she was prepared.
Hjörvarðr jarl vildi gjarna þetta til vinna, at hon kæmist á braut sem skjótast, því at honum þótti, sem var, mikil vandræði af standa hennar ráði.	Hjorvard the-earl willed gladly this to grant, that she comes to away as quickly, therefore that he thought, that was, much difficulty of standing her conduct.	Earl Hjorvard was glad to grant this so that she would go away as soon as possible, for he thought there was great difficulty with her conduct if she stayed.
Síðan lét hann búa at öllu þrjú langskip sem bezt.	Then had he prepared to all three longships as best.	Then he had prepared all three longships as best as possible.
En þegar þetta lið var búit, þá ferr Hléguðr jarlsdóttir ór landi með þessu liði ok lagðist síðan í hernað ok víking ok aflaði sér svá fjár ok frama.	Then as-soon-as the crew were prepared, then travelled Hlegunn the-earl's-daughter out-of land with this crew and lay afterwards to raiding and viking and obtained herself such wealth and fame.	Then as soon as the crew were ready Hlegunn the earl's daughter travelled out of the land with this crew and went raiding and viking and obtained such wealth and fame for herself.
Svá er sagt, at hon kom eigi í land, meðan faðir hennar lifði.	So was said, that she came not to land, while father hers lived.	So it was said that she did not come back to the land while her father lived.

The Tale of Star-Oddi's Dream (Old Norse)

Old Norse	Literal	English
En í annan stað er þar til at taka sögunnar, at þá er Geirviðr, sonr Hróðbjarts konungs, var átta vetra gamall, tók Hróðbjartr konungr sótt, ok verðr þat lítil frásaga, því at sóttin leiðir svá til lands, at konungrinn andast.	But in another place is there to of take the-saga, that then was Geirvid, son Hrodbjart's king, was eight winters old, took Hrodbjart king sickness, and became that little from-to-say, accordingly that sickness took so to the-lands, that the-king died.	But to take the saga to another place, then King Hrodbjart's son Geirvid was eight winters old, Hrodbjart took ill, and there was little to say of it, but a sickness took to the land and the king died.
Þat þótti öllum hans ástvinum ok virkðamönnum inn mesti skaði, sem var, at missa slíks höfðingja ok bar út í frá öllu landsfólkinu.	That thought all of-him beloved and chosen-man the most harm, as was, that missed such chieftains and there out to from all lands-folk.	Everyone thought this a great harm as he was beloved by his chosen companions, chieftains, and people of the land.
Síðan var fengit at virðuligri veizlu ok þar til boðit öllum inum ríkustum mönnum ok inum beztum höfðingjum, er í váru landinu.	Afterwards was got then worthy feast and there to invited all the kingdom's people and the best chieftains, that in were the-land.	Afterwards a worthy feast was prepared, and all of the kingdom's people and the best chieftains in the land were invited.
Þar með var ok til boðit hverjum manni, þeim er veizluna vildi sækja, bæði innan lands ok útan, svá at engi skyldi þar óboðit koma.	Then with was also to invited each person, they of feast willed seek, both within lands and without, so that none should there uninvited come.	With that, everyone who wished to attend was also invited, both within the land and without, so that no one should come uninvited.
En síðan þessi veizla var saman sett með því fjölmenni, er þangat sótti, þá var þar erfi drukkit eftir Hróðbjart konung með miklum veg ok sóma, svá sem byrjaði hans tígn ok sómasamligri virðingu.	Then after the feast were together set with because followers, were there attending, then was there a-toast drunk after Hrodbjart the-king with much way and honour, so as began his prestige and respectable worthiness.	Then after the feast was held with the many followers who attended there, a toast was drunk for King Hrodbjart, in such a way that honoured his prestige and respectable worthiness.
En er erfinu var lokit, þá var konungrinn heygðr at fornum sið eftir því, sem þá var tízka til við göfga menn.	Then as the-toast was ended, then was the-king buried in ancient traditions after according-to, as then was fashion to with noble men.	Then when the toast had ended, the king was buried according to ancient traditions that were then fashionable with noble men.

The Tale of Star-Oddi's Dream (Old Norse)

Old Norse	Literal	English
## 3	## 3	## 3
Nú er svá at segja, at eftir þessi miklu tíðendi, er þar í landi höfðu gerzt, þá sýndist þat öllum inum vitrustum mönnum ok inum beztum vinum konungsins at taka annan mann til konungs ok landstjórnar í stað þvílíks höfðingja, sem þá var við misst.	Now is so to say, that after this much news, was there in the-land had done, then seemed that all the-others wise people and the best friends the-king's to take another person to king and governing the place such-like chieftains, as then were with lost.	Now the saga goes that after this there was much news in the land that all the wise people and the king's best friends had to take another person as king and for the chieftains to cover the place as such a leader had been lost.
En svá var mikil ástúð öllum landsmönnum á Hróðbjarti konungi, meðan hann lifði, at menn vildu ekki annat en velja Geirvið, son hans, til konungs ok láta eigi konungdóminn ganga ór hans ætt.	But so was great affection of-all lands-people to Hrodbjart the-king, while he lived, that people willed not another to choose Geirvid, son his, to king and allowed not kingdom going out-of his lineage.	But so great was the affection of all the people of the land to King Hrodbjart while he lived that no one wanted to choose other than Geirvid his son as king and not to let the kingdom pass out of his lineage.
Þótt Geirviðr væri ungr at aldri eða hann þætti þá enn lítt til landráða fallinn í þann tíma, vildi þó allt landsfólkit til þessa hætta með umsjá dróttningar, móður hans, með því at hon var in vitrasta kona ok vel at sér í alla staði.	Thought Geirvid was young in age and he thought then that little to land-ruling disposed in that time, willed though all the-land's-people to this conclude with supervision queen, mother his, with accordingly that she was the wisest woman and well to herself in all places.	Though Geirvid was young in age and seemed little disposed to ruling the land at that time, all the people of the land wished it, with supervision of his mother the queen accordingly, as she was the wisest woman and capable in all ways.
En er svá fór fram um hríð, at svá ungr maðr skyldi höfðingi vera ok stjórna mörgu fólki sem Geirviðr var, þá gerðist brátt landsstjórnin lítil, sem líkligt var.	But when so went from about awhile, that so young man should chieftain be and ruling many folk as Geirvid was, then became soon the-government little, as likely was.	But when this had been so for a while, with such a young man as Geirvid being a ruler and governing many people, then the government became weak, as was likely.
Þat gerðist ok, at hirðin fátkaðist, fyrir því at margir váru þeir af hans hirðmönnum, at aðra iðn lögðu fyrir sik.	It became also, that courtiers few, because therefore that many were they of his court-men, that other crafts laid for themselves.	It also came about that he courtiers were fewer because many of his court men found themselves other jobs.
Sumir lögðust í víking, aðrir réðust í kaupferðir til ýmissa landa.	Some laid to viking-raids, others appointed to merchant-voyages to various lands.	Some went on viking raids, others were appointed on merchant voyages to various lands.

The Tale of Star-Oddi's Dream (Old Norse)

Old Norse	Literal	English
Nú með því at á þessu þótti mikit mein, sem nú var frá sagt, þá gerðust þó mörg önnur óhægendi í ríki þessa ins unga konungs.	Now with therefore that of this thought much harm, as how was from said, then made though many others inconvenience in the-kingdom this the young king.	Now with this being thought of as much harm, as before said, then there were other inconveniences in the kingdom of this young kind.
Þess er við getit í sögunni, at illvirkjar tveir lögðust út á skóg þann, er Jöruskógr heitir.	This was with told-of in the-saga, that evil-doers two camped out in forest then, was Battle-forest named.	It was told of in this saga that two evil doers camped out in the forest which was then named Battle Forest.
Þat var í ríki þessa ins unga manns.	It was in kingdom this the young man's.	This was in the young man's kingdom.
Þessir víkingar drápu menn til fjár sér ok váru náliga berserkir.	These vikings killed people for wealth as also were nearly berserkers.	These vikings killed men for money and were virtually berserkers.
Annarr þeira hét Garpr, en annarr Gnýr.	One of-them named Garp, and the-other Gny.	One of them was named Garp, and the other Gny.
Svá er sagt, at mönnum hlýddi aldri fám at fara saman.	So is said, that people followed never few to travel together.	So it was said that people never travelled in small numbers together.
Jafnan váru menn vanir at fara á skóginn með fjölmenni at leita illvirkjanna ok ráða þá af, en þeir urðu aldrigi hittir, þó at þeira væri leita farit með fjölmenni.	Always were people friends that travelled to the-forest with followers-many to search for-the-evil-doers and prevail then of, which they became never found, though that they were searching travelling with followers-many.	People were always travelling with friends to the forest with followers to search for these evil doers and defeat them, but they were never found, even though many people were searching for them.
Slíku ferr fram, til þess er Geirviðr konungr er tólf vetra.	So it-went from, to this that Geirvid the-king was twelve winters.	So it went on until King Geirvid was twelve winters old.
Ok þá er hann var svá aldrs kominn, þá var hann svá mikill maðr vexti ok sterkr at afli sem þeir menn margir, sem fullkomnir váru at aldri ok atgervi náliga, eftir því sem þeir bezt váru á sik komnir fyrir allra hluta sakir.	And then when he was so of-age come, then was he so much a-man grown and strong in strength as they men many, as fully-come were to age and deeds closely, after accordingly which they best were in himself come before all things sake.	And then when he had come of age, he was a great man in height and strength, as much as many men who had come of age, and almost like those who were at their peak in all things.

The Tale of Star-Oddi's Dream (Old Norse)

Old Norse	Literal	English
Þat var eitthvert sinn, þá er Geirviðr konungr sat yfir borðum með allri hirð sinni, þá tók hann til orða ok mælti svá:	Then was some-time one-day, then that Geirvid the-king sat over the-tables with all retainers his, then took he to words and spoke so:	Then one day King Geirvid sat at the table with his retainers, and took to words and said:
Nú er svá sem yðr er kunnigt, öllum mínum mönnum, at ek hefi ungr verit hér til at aldri, ok svá hefi ek haft litla orku, ok því hefir af mér staðit lítil stjórn í ríkinu.	Now is so as you that known, all my men, that I have young been forces to that age, and so have I had little power, and therefore have of me stood little control in the-kingdom.	Now it is well known to you, all my people, that I have been young and have had little power, and therefore I have had little control over the kingdom.
Hefi ek þat ok oft heyrt, sem ván er at.	Have I that and often heard, as expected was it.	And I have often heard, as was expected,
Má þat ok eigi mjök undrast, þó at hér til hafi af mér lítil stjórn staðit fyrir sakir æsku minnar.	May it also not much wonder, though that forces to have of me little control placed before the-sake-of youth mine.	It may also not be much to wonder that I have had little force of control for the sake of my youth.
En þó er ek nú svá aldrskominn, at mér er nú mál at reyna mik ok vita, at nökkut vili mitt ráð þroskast ok meir hefjast en áðr er, þar sem ek er nú orðinn maðr tólf vetra gamall.	However though am I now so come-of-age, that to-me is now matter to test myself and know, that something wish mine decide develop and more start then after that, there was I am now become a-man twelve winters old.	However, now that I have come of age, there is now the matter to test myself and I wish to know something whether it is decided that my rule will develop and become more after than it was at the start, now that I am a man of twelve winters old.
Eru ok margir ekki betr mannaðir á mínum aldri.	Are and many not better mannered at my age.	There are many my age who are not better mannered than me.
Nú vil ek ok því lýsa fyrir öllum yðr, mínum þegnum ok virðavinum, at ek ætla mér at fara til móts við berserkina, þá Garp ok Gný, er liggja á Jöruskógi ok gera þar mörg illvirki.	Now will I also therefore show for all of-you, my subjects and friends, that I intend me to travel to meet with berserkers, then Garp and Gny, who camped in Battle-forest and do there many outrages.	Now therefore I wish to show all of you, my subjects and friends, that I intend to travel to meet with the berserkers, Garp and Gny, who camp in Battle Forest and do many outrages there.
Ætla ek ok til þess at koma eigi aftr svá, at þeir sé á lífi, ok skal ek þá yfirkoma eða þeir mik ella",	Intend I also to this that come not back so, so-as they are of alive, and shall I then overcome or they me or-else",	I also do not intend to come back so long as they are alive, and either I shall over come them, or they me".

The Tale of Star-Oddi's Dream (Old Norse)

Old Norse	Literal	English
En er Geirviðr konungr hafði þetta mælt, þá svarar fyrst máli hans dróttningin, móðir hans, ok þar með allir hans beztu menn, ok mæltu náliga allir sem eins manns munni ok báðu konung fara fjölmennan á fund stigamannanna ok með miklum viðbúnaði, ef hann vildi fara.	And when Geirvid the-king had this spoke, then answered first speech his the-queen, mother his, and there with all his best people, and spoke almost all as one man's mouth and asked the-king travel followers-many to find the-robbing-men and with much preparation, if he wished to-travel.	And when King Geirvid had spoken, the first to answer his speech was his mother the queen, along with his best people, and all spoke almost with one voice and asked that the king travel with many followers to find the robbing men and with much preparation if he wished to travel.
Geirviðr konungr svarar:	Geirvid the-king answered:	King Geirvid answered:
Hugsat hefi ek þetta mál áðr nökkut fyrir mér en ek kvæða upp, ok sýnist mér á þá leið sem í þessari ferð megi mér þá engi frami kaupast, þótt ek fá nát berserkjunum, enda leita ek þeira með miklu liði alvápnuðu,	Think have I this matter before some-time for me that I announced up, and seems to-me that then passes so in this journey may for-me then not courage redeem, though I get protection the-berserkers, with seeking I them with much company all-weaponed,	I have been thinking about this matter for some time before I announced it and it seems to me that if it so passes on my journey, I may not redeem courage if I have the protection from the berserkers while seeking them with a great company all armed.
en þat er þá nökkur svívirðing, ef þeir fást þá eigi ok koma ek við þat aftr, ok verðr þá ósnöfrmannliga minnar handar, ef svá tekst.	but it is then somewhat disgraceful, if them get then not and come I with it returning, and became then un-alert my hand, if so takes.	But then it is a disgrace if they are not caught, and I will come to return, and then it will have been feeble for my hand if it it ends like that.
Nú hefi ek hina leið ætlat ferðina at fara með annan mann á þeira fund, ok mun þá skipta gæfa með oss, hverr þá skal verða várr skilnaðr.	Now have I then company intend travelling that travel with another person that they find, and should then exchange good-fortune with us, each then shall become our parting.	Now I intend to travel with another person to find them, and it should then exchange good fortune between us and we shall se how we part.
Má þá ok verða, ef vill, at nökkur svá fremð fylgi ferðinni.	May then also be, if will, that something so honour follows the-journey.	May it then also become, if willing, that some honour follows this journey.
Skal nú ok á þat ráð hætta, hversu sem til vill takast.	Shall now also to that decide conclude, how-so as to will take.	That shall now decide and conclude how it may turn out.

The Tale of Star-Oddi's Dream (Old Norse)

Old Norse	Literal	English
Er nú ok fyrir því upp borit þetta mál fyrir yðr, at ek vil nú vita, hverr fúsastr er til þessarar ferðar með mér, ok er nú þat ráð, at nökkurr vakni við, sá er til vill ráðast, ok svari sá nú mínu máli, enda skuluð þér þat vita hér með, at nú er þetta mál fullgert fyrir mína hönd, at ek mun þó fara þessa ferð, þótt ek fara einn saman ok verði engi til at fylgja mér",	Is now also before because up brought this matter before you, that I wish no to-know, who willing that to this journey with me, and is now that decision, to someone wake against, so that to wish arrange, and answer so now my speech, and should you it know here with, that now is this matter full-done before my hand, that I should though travel this journey, though I travel one the-same and be none to that follow me",	Now, therefore, this matter has been brought before you that I now want to know who is most willing to go on this journey with me, and it is now the plan that someone will wake up, whoever may decide, and he will now answer my question, and you shall do so. Know herewith that now this matter is settled on my behalf that I will still go on this journey even though I go alone and there will be no one to follow me".
En við þessi ummæli konungs, þá er þat sagt, at dróttning sjálf fyrst at upphafi latti á alla vega þessar ferðar ok sagði, sem var, allbráðliga stofnat, þar sem við heljarmenn var at eiga, er illvirkjarnir váru, svá mikit sem þar var í ábyrgð, er konungrinn var sjálfr, því at öllum þótti viss ván, at hann mundi látast fyrir þeim ok fá minna hlut í þeira skiptum, ef svá yrði sem líkligt mundi þykkja fyrir sakir æsku konungs þeira, en harðfengi berserkjanna.	And with these about-words the-king's, then was it said, that the-queen herself first to became discouraged to all ways this journey and said, that was, all-un-forethought planned, there as with accursed-men was that only, were criminals were, so much as there was in responsibility, was the-king's was himself, therefore to all thought aware expecting, that he would die before them and get less lot of there exchanged, if so became as likely would regarded for sake youth the-king's they, which toughness the-berserkers.	And with these words from the king, then it was said that the queen herself was the first to discourage this expedition in every respect, and she said it had been planned with little forethought, with these accursed men who were criminals, as much as there was a responsibility for the king himself, all expected that he would get the worst of it and die because of them, if it became as was likely, for the sake of the king's youth and the toughness of the berserkers.
Allir vinir konungs löttu ákafliga fararinnar ok þótti konungr út seldr, ef hann færi við annan mann.	All friends the-king's dissuaded extremely of-the-journey and thought the-king out sold, if he journeyed with another man.	All the king's friends were extremely discouraging of the journey and thought that the king would be done for if he went with only one other man.
Konungr svarar, at ekki mundi tjóa at letja hann.	The-king answered, that not would avail to discourage him.	The king answered that it would be to no avail to try and discourage him.
Ok er allir skilðu, at konungr mundi eigi letjast láta, þá verðr til ok svarar máli konungs sá, er Dagfinnr hét.	And when all knew, that the-king would not discouraged allow, then became to also answer the-matter the-king's so, that Dagfinn named.	And when all understood that the king would not be discouraged, then cane an answer to the king's case, who was named Dagfinn.

The Tale of Star-Oddi's Dream (Old Norse)

Old Norse	Literal	English
Hann var hirðmaðr konungs ok konungsskáld.	He was court-man the-king's and the-king's-poet.	He was the king's court man and the king's poet.
"Herra", segir hann, "engan mann veit ek þér meiri sæmð eiga at launa í alla staði en mik.	"Lord", said he, "no person know I to-you more honour have to reward in all places than me.	"Lord," said he, "I know of no man more honorable to you in all things than me.
Er ek ok því skyldari at skiljast aldri við þik, er þú ert í meira háska staddr, ef þér vilið þiggja mitt föruneyti ok fylgð, ok er ek til þessar farar albúinn, þegar þér vilið",	Am I also therefore obliged to separate never with you, that you are the more danger placed, if you wish accept my companionship and follow, and that I to this travel all-prepared, as-soon-as you wish",	I am therefore more obliged to never part with you when you are in more danger if you want to accept my entourage and escort, and I am ready for this journey whenever you want".

4

En þegar þessi maðr, Dagfinnr, var nefndr í sögunni, þá er frá því at segja, er mjök er undarligt, at þá brá því við í drauminum Odda, at hann Oddi sjálfr þóttist vera þessi maðr, Dagfinnr, en gestrinn, sá er söguna sagði, er nú ór sögunni ok drauminum, en þá þóttist hann sjálfr sjá ok vita allt þat, er heðan af er í drauminum.	Then as-soon-as this man, Dagfinn, was named in the-saga, then was from accordingly to say, that much was wonder-like, that then drew therefore with in the-dream Oddi's, that he Oddi himself thought was this man, Dagfinn, but-the-guest, so was the-saga telling, was now out-of the-saga and the-dream, and then thought he himself so and knew all that, was from-here of for in the-dream.	But when this man, Dagfinn, was mentioned in the story, it is very strange to say that in Oddi's dream it happened that Oddi himself thought he was this man, Dagfinn, but the guest who told the story is now out of the story and the dream, but then he thought he saw and knew all that is henceforth in the dream.
En nú síðan er drauminn svá at segja sem honum þótti sjálfum fyrir sik bera, Odda, þá þóttist hann vera Dagfinnr ok ráðast í ferðina með konunginum Geirviði.	Then now after in the-dream so to say as he thought himself before himself borne, Oddi, then thought he was Dagfinn and arranging to travel with the-king Geirvid.	But now since the dream is, so to speak, that Oddi then he thought he was Dagfinn and embarked on the journey with King Geirvid.

The Tale of Star-Oddi's Dream (Old Norse)

Old Norse	Literal	English
En er þeir váru albúnir, þá riðu þeir tveir saman með vápnum sínum, til þess er þeir kómu á Jöruskóg, þangat sem illvirkjanna var ván, en þar var svá við vaxit, at gata var breið um skóginn,	Then when they were all-prepared, then rode they two together with weapons theirs, to this that they came to Battle-forest, from-there as the-evil-doers were expecting, then they were so trees grown, that the-way was broad about the-forest,	Then when they were ready the two rode together with their weapons until they came to Battle Forest, where the evil doers were waiting, then the trees were so grown that there was a wide path through the forest.
ok er þeir kómu mjök langt í skóginn, þá er þess getit, at þar varð fyrir þeim hóll einn mjök hár.	and when they came much long in the-forest, then is this told-of, that there was before them hill one much high.	And when they came very far into the forest, it is told that there was a very high hill before them.
Hann var brattr öllum megin.	It was broad all sides.	It was steep on all sides.
Síðan gengu þeir upp á hólinn ok vildu þaðan sjást um ok vita, hverra tíðenda þeir mætti vissir verða.	Afterwards went they up by the-hill and wished then t-look about and know, what news they may know to-be.	Then they went up the hill and from there wanted to look around and know what tidings they might become.
Margt smágrjót var á hóli þessum.	Many small-stones were on hill this.	Many small stones were on this hill.
Þaðan sá þeir víða.	From-there saw they widely.	From there they saw widely.
Þeir geta at líta, hvar ganga tveir menn.	They could to look, where going two men.	They could see where the two men were walking.
Þeir váru miklir vexti ok gengu þegar þangat at hólinum, sem þeir konungr stóðu.	They were great grown and went they from-there to the-hill, as they the-king stood.	They were tall and they immediately walked to the hill where the king stood.
Þessir menn váru báðir vel vápnaðir.	These men were both well weaponed.	These men were both well armed.
En þegar þeir konungr ok Dagfinnr sá þessa menn, þá þóttust þeir vita, at þar váru þeir komnir, Garpr ok Gnýr.	Then as-soon-as they the-king and Dagfinn saw these men, then thought they knew, that there were they coming, Garp and Gny.	But when the king and Dagfinn saw these men, they thought they knew that Garp and Gny had come there.
Þá mælti Dagfinnr:	Then spoke Dagfinn:	Then Dagfinn said,

The Tale of Star-Oddi's Dream (Old Norse)

Old Norse	Literal	English
Herra, ek vil yðr kunnigt gera, at ek er eigi mjök vanr vápnaskipti, ok kann ek lítt at treysta hug mínum né vápnfimi.	Lord, I wish to-you know be, that I am not much accustomed weapons-exchange, and can I a-little to trust mind mine nor weapon-nimble.	Lord, I want to let you know that I am not very accustomed to exchanging arms, and I can scarcely trust my mind or my agility.
Nú vil ek, at þér kjósið um tvá kosti, hvárt þér vilið heldr, at ek ráðist mót berserkjunum með þér, eða villtu, at ek sjá til yðvarrar sameignar af hólinum ok kunna ek frá at segja öðrum mönnum",	Now wish I, that you choose about two benefits, either you wish rather, that I determine-to meet the-berserkers with you, or will-you, that I see that your fight of the-hill and know I from to say to-other people",	Now I want you to choose two options, whether you want me to attack the berserkers with you or you want me to see to your fight from the hill and I can tell other people what happened".
Konungr svarar:	The-king answered:	The king answered:
Ef þér lér nökkut tveggja huga um þetta mál, þá þykkir mér einsætt, at þú sér hér á hólinum ok sjáir heðan til sameignar várrar ok komir eigi nær við vár vápnaskipti",	If you lean somewhat two minds about this matter, then seems to-me evident, that you are here on the-hill and look from-here to the-fight aware and come not near with our weapons-exchange",	If you lean somewhat in two minds about this matter, I think it is decided that you are here on the hill and see from here to the fight and do not come any closer to our exchange of arms.
Dagfinnr tekr þat ráð, sem konungr mælti, ok dvaldist eftir á hólinum ok kemr hvergi nær, ok þykkir honum þat allráðligt, en konungrinn sjálfr ræðst ofan af hólinum í móti stigamönnum.	Dagfinn took this advice, as the-king spoke, and dwelled afterwards on the-hill and came each near, and seemed to-him that advisable, what the-king himself decided over of the-hill in meeting the-robbers.	Dagfinn took the advice which the king had said and stayed on the hill, and came nowhere near, and he thought it wise, but the king himself attacked from the top of the hill against the robbers.
Þar kann eigi glöggliga frá at segja, hversu högg fóru með þeim, ok mun ek þar gera skjóta frásögu, því at þat er þar frá lyköum at segja, at svá skipti hamingjan með þeim, því at konungi var lagit líf ok lykka, at hann bar af báðum illvirkjunum, ok létust þeir af stórum sárum, er konungr hafði þeim veitt.	There known not clearly from to say, how-so blows went between them, and should I there do short from-saying, because that it was there from completion to say, that so exchanged graciousness with them, because that the-king was granted life and luck, that he bore of both evil-doers, and had they of great wounds, that the-king had them given.	It is not clear from there how the blows went with them, and I will make a quick account of it, for it is from there to say that their happiness that was so important to them was exchanged, for the king was given life and happiness, that he bore from both evil doers. and they died of the great wounds which the king had inflicted on them.

The Tale of Star-Oddi's Dream (Old Norse)

Old Norse	Literal	English
Ok eftir þat er illvirkjarnir váru fallnir, þá gengu þeir konungr ok Dagfinnr fram á götuna lengra ok kómu þar at farandi, er stígr lítill lá af þjóðbrautinni í skóginn.	And afterwards that when the-evil-doers were fallen, then went they the-king and Dagfinn from to path longer and came there to travel, where climbed little lying of the-highway in the-forest.	And after the evildoers had fallen, the king and Dagfinn went further out into the path, and came to a place where a small path lay from the highway into the forest.
Þeir höfðu litla stund gengit þann inn litla stíg, áðr brátt gerðist rjóðr mjök mikit í mörkinni, ok stóð þar eitt hús.	They had little awhile gone then the little path, before soon became clearing much greatly in the-border, and stood there one house.	They had walked the small path for a short time before soon there was a lot of clearing in the border and a house stood there.
Þat hús var hátt ok rammgert ok læst ok grafinn lykill í dyrigætti.	The house was tall and firmly-built and locked and the-key buried in doorway.	That house was tall and firmly built, and firmly locked with a key buried in the doorway.
Þeir luku upp húsinu ok gengu þar inn.	They unlocked up the-house and went they in.	They opened the house and went inside.
Þat hús var vel innan búit ok var náliga fullt af alls kyns auðæfum.	The house was well inside prepared and was nearly full of all kinds-of wealthy-treasures.	That house was well furnished and was almost full of all kinds of riches.
Þar váru þeir um nóttina, ok skorti þar hvárki góðan drykk né dýran mat, en um morgininn fóru þeir heimleiðis, ok huldu áðr hræ útilegumannanna.	They were there about the-night, and shortage of neither good drink nor fine food, then about morning travelled they homeward, and covering after corpses the-outlaw-men.	They were there during the night and there was no shortage of good drinks or expensive food, but in the morning they went home and hid the carcasses of the outlaw men before.
En er konungrinn kom heim til ríkis síns, þá varð hann frægr mjök víða um lönd af sínu þrekvirki ok ágætum sigri, ok urðu allir vinir konungsins ok frændr honum fegnir, er hann kom heim með göfugligum sigri, ok þóttust menn hann náliga ór helju heimt hafa, sem var.	Then when the-king came home to kingdom his, then was he famous much with about the-land of his brave-deeds and wonderful victory, and became all friends the-king's and kinsmen his celebrated, that he came home with noble-like victory, and thought people he nearly out-of Hel drawn had, as was.	But when the king came home to his kingdom, he became famous in many lands for his endurance and excellent victory, and all the king's friends and relatives rejoiced when he came home with a noble victory, and it was thought that people had almost recovered him from hell, which they were.

The Tale of Star-Oddi's Dream (Old Norse)

Old Norse	Literal	English
## 5	## 5	## 5
Nú eftir þenna atburð allan saman lét konungr þings kveðja, ok kemr þar mikit fjölmenni saman.	Now after these events all together had the-king an-assembly called, and came there great many-followers together.	Now after all these events, the king called an assembly and a great many people gathered there.
En er saman var sett þetta it fjölmenna þing, þá sagði konungr þar þessi miklu tíðendi, ok þótti öllum þetta in mesta frægð, sem var, er Geirviðr konungr hafði einn sigr borit af slíkum kempum.	Then when together were sat that the many-men the-assembly, then said the-king there this great news, and thought all this the most fame, which was, that Geirvid the-king had one victory carried of such champion.	And when this large assembly was convened, the king there told this great news, and it was considered by all to be the greatest fame, which was that King Geirvid had won one such a battle.
Síðan bað Geirviðr, at menn skyldi vitja til þess húss, er illvirkjarnir höfðu í borit þat mikla fé, ok skyldi þar hverr taka sitt fé, þat er misst hafði,	Afterwards invited Geirvid, that people should visit to the house, where the-evil-doers had in bore that much wealth, and should there each take his wealth, that was missed had,	Then Geirvid asked that men should visit the house in which the evildoers had brought much money, and that each should take his money which he had lost.
en allir gáfu konungi upp sitt fé, þat sem hverr átti, ok sögðu þat bezt komit, at hann hefði, ok kváðu hann fullu kostat hafa.	but all have the-king up their wealth, that which each had, and said that best came, to him have, and said he fully earned had.	But they all gave to the king what they had, and said that it was best for him to have it, and said that he had earned it in full.
Síðan lét konungr sækja féit ok kastaði á sinni eigu.	Afterwards had the-king sought the-treasure and cast to his ownership.	Then the king fetched the money and cast it into his possession.
Eftir þat lét konungr taka til húsgerðar, ok gerðu menn konungi haug þann, er hann skyldi sitja á.	After that had the-king taken to house-builder, and made people the-king a-mound then, that he should sit on.	After that the king had a house built, and the people made a mound for the king to sit on.
Þá var konungr settr á stól þann, er stóð á hauginum, ok hófu menn hann svá einkum til tígnar ok gáfu honum þá enn af nýju dýrar presentur ok dýrkuðu hann, sem þeir höfðu framast föng á.	Then was the-king sat on throne then, as place on the-mound, and had people him so especially to princely and gave him then but of new precious presents and adored him, as they had foremost possessions of.	Then the king was placed on the throne that stood on the mound, and the people began to honor him, and gave him again expensive gifts, and worshiped him whom they had bestowed.

The Tale of Star-Oddi's Dream (Old Norse)

Old Norse	Literal	English
Þess er við getit, þar sem Dagfinnr skáld er, honum kom í hug, at engi mundi skyldari til konunginn at sæma með kvæði en svá sem hann var.	This is with told-of, that as Dagfinn the-poet was, he came to mind, that none would obliged to the-king to honour with a-poem than such as he was.	This is told of Dagfinn the poet, that it occurred to him that no one would be more obliged to the king to honour with a poem than he was.
Síðan gengr Dagfinnr á hauginn upp til konungsins ok fell á kné fyrir hann ok laut honum ok kvaddi hann virðuliga ok sagði honum, at hann hefði kvæði ort um konunginn, ok bað, at hann mundi hlýða.	Afterwards went Dagfinn on the-mound up to the-king and fell to knee before him and place his and greeted him worthily and said to-him, that he had a-poem worded about the-king, and asked, that he would listen.	Then Dagfinn went to the mound up to the king and fell on his knees before him and bowed to him and greeted him respectfully and told him that he had written a poem about the king and asked him to listen.
Konungr játti því blíðliga.	King said accordingly joyfully.	The king agreed joyfully.
Síðan tók Dagfinnr til ok flutti kvæðit, ok var þat flokkr.	Then took Dagfinn to and brought the-poem, and was it flokk.	Then Dagfinn took over and performed the poem, and it was a flokk.
Ok er lokit var kvæðinu, þá þakkar konungr vel ok allir þeir, er við váru staddir, ok sögðu vel ort ok svá sem sæmði tígn ok virðing konungs þeira.	And when ended was the-poem, then thanked the-king well and all there, was with were standing, and said well worded and so as honour prestige and worthy king they.	And when the poem was finished, the king thanked well and all those who were present and said it was well written and so they honored the prestige and worthiness of their king.
Ok sem konungr heyrði, at allir létu vel yfir ok lofuðu mjök kvæðit, þá vildi hann sér láta ok verða stórmannliga ok launa höfðingliga ok vill gefa skáldinu gullhring mikinn, er hann hafði á arminum,	And as the-king heard, that all had all over and praised much the-poem, then willed he himself to-have and worthy great-man-like and reward nobly and wanted-to give the-poet a-gold-ring great, that he had on arm,	And when the king heard that everyone had praised the poem very much, he wanted to be generous and reward the poet with a large gold ring that he had on his arm.
en Dagfinnr vildi eigi hringinn þiggja ok sagði svá, at honum var mikil aufúsa á því at hafa sóma ok virðing af konunginum, en fé kvaðst hann eigi þurfa at þiggja af honum ok kallaði sik ekki skorta, meðan hann heldi honum heilum,	but Dagfinn wished not the-ring accept and said so, that he was great gratitude that therefore to have honour and worth of the-king, that treasure said he not needed to accept of him and claimed himself not shortage, while he held him whole,	But Dagfinn did not wish to accept the ring and said that he was very grateful to have the honour and respect of the king, but he said he did not need to accept it from him because he had no shortage of anything as long as he kept him safe,
"en þeir eru margir aðrir, er þar sjá til fjárins, sem þér eruð",	"but there are many others, that there look to wealth, as to-you are",	but there are any others who look for wealth while looking to you.

The Tale of Star-Oddi's Dream (Old Norse)

Old Norse	Literal	English
Konungi líkar þetta vel.	The-king liked this well.	This pleased the king.

6

Old Norse	Literal	English
Þessu næst er at segja frá þeim tíðendum, at Hjörguðr, kona Hjörvarðar jarls, tók sótt hættliga, ok þarf þar eigi at gera mikinn orðahjaldr, at þessi sótt leiðir Hjörgunni til bana.	This next was to say from they news, that Hjorgunn, wife-of Hjorvard the-earl, took sickness dangerously, and needed there not to do much word-struggle, that this sickness took Hjorgunn to death.	The next thing to tell of news was that Hjorgunn, the wife of Earl Hjorvard, took a dangerous sickness and there is no need to struggle with words to say that this sickness took Hjorgunn to her death.
Síðan var hon erfð ok út borin ok gert eftir hana sem tízka var til í fornum sið eftir ríkar konur.	Afterwards was she honoured and out brought and made after her as fashion was to in ancient traditions after rich women.	Afterwards she was honoured and brought out and so it was done for her in the fashion of ancient traditions of wealthy women.
Jarli þótti mikill skaði eftir dróttning sína, sem ván var, ok harmaði hana mjök ok svá margir aðrir út í frá.	The-earl thought much harm after the-queen himself, as expected was, and mourned her much and so many others out in from.	The earl thought great harm to his queen, which was expected, and mourned her greatly, along with so many others from then on.
Eigi höfðu liðit langir tímar, áðr vinir hans fýstu, at hann skyldi fá sér annarrar konu.	Not had passed long time, before friends his urged, that he should get himself another wife.	It had not been long before his friends wanted him to have another wife.
Hann spurði, hvar þeir sæi honum kvánfang þat, er honum væri virðing í at fá.	He asked, where they saw him a-match that, was to-him being worthy in to get.	He asked where they saw for him a wife that he would be honored to receive.
Þeir tölðu ráðligt, at hann bæði til handa sér Hildigunnar dróttningar, ok sögðu honum mikit uppheldi at þeim ráðahag, ef hann næðist.	They told advice, that he ask for the-hand he Hildigunn the-queen, and said to-him much advancement that they marriage-proposal, if he reached.	They thought it advisable for him to ask for the hand of Queen Hildigunn, and said that there would be much advancement for him if such a marriage could be achieved.
Ok er þetta var oft tját fyrir jarli, þá sýndist á þá leið, því at hann var vitr maðr.	And was that was often expressed before the-earl, then seemed to then laid, therefore that he was wise man.	And when this was often told to the earl, he saw things the same way, because he was a wise man.
Síðan hefir hann upp orð sín ok biðr Hildigunnar dróttningar sér til eiginkonu.	Afterwards had he up worded his and invited Hildigunn the-queen herself to wife.	Then he raised his words and asked Queen Hildigunn to marry him.

The Tale of Star-Oddi's Dream (Old Norse)

Old Norse	Literal	English
Hon var þá enn ekki meir en fertug kona at aldri, ok þótti kostrinn vera inn merkiligsti fyrir allra hluta sakir.	She was then was not more than forty woman in age, and thought distinguished was the remarkable before all things sake.	She was still no more than forty women at the time and was considered the most remarkable option for all intents and purposes.
Ok hvárt sem um þetta var talat lengr eða skemr, þá var þat at ráði gert, at dróttning var gift Hjörvarði jarli með ráði konungs, sonar hennar.	And how as about this was told longer or shorter, then was it that decision made, that the-queen was married Hjorvard the-earl with consent the-king, son hers.	And whether this was talked about longer or shorter, it was decided that the queen should marry Earl Hjorvard, with the consent of her son the king.
Síðan var fengit at virðuligri veizlu ok drukkit brúðhlaup Hjörvarðar jarls ok Hildigunnar dróttningar með miklum veg ok margs konar sóma.	Afterwards was got a worthy feast and drank the-wedding Hjorvard the-earl and Hildigunn the-queen with much way and many kinds-of honour.	Then a worthy feast was held, and the wedding of Earl Hjörvarður and Queen Hildigunn was drunk with great prestige and many honours.
Ok er veizlunni var lokit, þá ferr hverr heim til sinna heimkynna.	And when the-feast was concluded, then travelled each home to their households.	And when the feast was over, everyone went home to their households.
Brátt takast þar miklar ástir í millum þeira, ok eru samfarar þeira sæmiligar ok eigi langar, áðr en þau áttu dóttur.	Soon took there much love in between them, and was interaction theirs honourable and not long, after then they had a-daughter.	Soon there was much love between them and their interaction was honourable, and it was not long after that they had a daughter.
Hon var nefnd Hlaðreið.	She was named Hladreid.	She was named Hladreid.
Svá er sagt, at samför þeira jarls ok dróttningar var eigi löng þaðan í frá, er þau höfðu Hlaðreiði getit, áðr þau tíðendi gerðust, at jarl tekr sótt, ok leiðir hon svá til lands, at hann andast af þeiri sótt.	So was said, that togetherness theirs the-earl and the-queen was not long from-there to from, when they had Hladreid told, before the news made, that earl took sickness, and led it so to the-land, that he died of that sickness.	So it was said that the togetherness of the earl and the queen did not last long after they had Hladreid, before the news came that the earl had taken ill, and so it led through the land, and he died of that sickness.
Þat þótti vera skaði mikill, því at hann var virðuligr höfðingi.	It thought was harm much, because that he was worthy chieftain.	It was thought a great harm because he was a worthy chieftain.
Eftir þessi tíðendi setti Geirviðr konungr sína menn yfir ríkit, þat er jarl hafði átt, ok eignaði sér.	After this the-news set Geirvid the-king his men over the-kingdom, that the earl had owned, and owned himself.	After these tidings King Geirvid put his men over the kingdom which the earl had owned and appropriated.

The Tale of Star-Oddi's Dream (Old Norse)

Old Norse	Literal	English
Þessi tíðendi spyrjast víða, sem ván var, fráfall þvílíks höfðingja.	This news was-heard widely, as expected was, death such-like a-chieftain.	These tidings were widely learned of, as was to be expected, from the demise of such a ruler.
Þar kemr, at þessi tíðendi koma fyrir Hlégunni, dóttur Hjörvarðar jarls, at faðir hennar er andaðr, þar sem hon er í hernaði ok brýtr undir sik víkinga.	There came, to this news came before Hlegunn, daughter Hjorvard the-earl, that father hers had died, there as she was about raiding and subduing under herself vikings.	There came these tidings to Hlegunn, the daughter of Earl Hjorvard, that her father was dead, as she was at war and subduing vikings.
Bregðr henni svá við tíðendin, at hon snýr öllu sínu liði til Gautlands ok herjar þar.	Reaction hers so with news, that she turned all her company to Götaland and raided there.	She reacted to the news by turning all her army towards Götaland and raided there.
Ok svá kemr því máli, at hon lagði undir sik allt þat ríki, er átt hafði faðir hennar.	And so came therefore the-matter, that she had under herself all that kingdom, which owned had father hers.	And then it came to pass that she subdued all the kingdom which her father had possessed.
Síðan sendir hon menn á fund Geirviðar konungs ok bað svá segja honum sín orð, at hann skyldi annathvárt gera at unna henni hálfs ríkis ok landráða við sjálfan sik eða ella skyldi hann búa sik ok sína menn ok koma til móts við hana með sinn her í sund þau, er heita Síldasund, ok berjast við hana þar, ok hefði þat þeira sigr ok gagn, er meiri gæfu stýrði.	Afterwards sent she men to find Geirvid the-king and asked to say to-him her words, that he should another-either do to grant her half the-kingdom and land-ruling with herself his or either should he prepare himself and his men and come to meet with her with her army in a-sound there, was named Herring-sound, and battle with her there, and had that there victory and won, was more luck guided.	Afterwards she sent men to find Geirvid and asked them to tell him her words, that he should either grant her half the kingdom and authority to rule or prepare himself and his men to come to meet with her army in a sound that was named Herringsound and battle with her there, and that victory would be won by whoever had the most luck.

7

Nú er þar til at taka, at sendimenn fóru, þeir er Hléguðr sendi.	Now is there to to take, the messengers travelled, they that Hlegunn sent.	Now we take to the messengers that Hlegunn had sent.
Þat váru skjaldmeyjar.	They were shield-maidens.	They were shield-maidens.
Þær fóru á konungs fund ok báru upp sín erendi fyrir konunginn.	They went to the-king meet and brought up their errand before the-king.	They went to meet the king and presented their message to the king.

The Tale of Star-Oddi's Dream (Old Norse)

Old Norse	Literal	English
Ok er hann heyrði kostaboð Hlégunnar, þá svarar hann skjótt á þessa leið:	And when he heard choice-bid Hlegunn's, then answered he quickly to this laid:	And when he heard Hlegunn's offer, he answered quickly in this way:
Því skjótara skal kjósa sem kostir eru ójafnari, ok vil ek miklu heldr berjast við hana en láta ríki mitt fyrir ágangi hennar",	Because shorter shall choices which choose they-are unequal, and will I much rather fight with her than lose kingdom mine before aggression hers",	I shall sooner choose the more unequal option, and I would much rather fight against it than leave my kingdom to its invasion.
Sendimenn fóru aftr á fund Hlégunnar ok segja henni til svá búins, ok líkaði henni þeira för forkunnliga vel.	Sending-men travelled returning to meet Hlegunn and said to-her to so prepared, and liked her their journey exceedingly well.	The messengers went back to meet Hlegunn and told her what had happened and she was pleased with their journey very much.
Nú er þat at segja, at Geirviðr konungr safnar herliði um allt sitt ríki, ok skal hverr maðr fara í þessa herför, er skildi má valda eða skafti skjóta.	Now is it to say, that Geirvid the-king gathered war-company about all his kingdom, and shall each man travel to this warfare, who shield may wield or spear throw.	Now it is said that King Geirvid gathered armies all over his kingdom, and every man should go on this campaign whether he can carry a shield or throw a spear.
Þess er við at geta, at höfði sá gekk einum megin hjá sundunum, er Hofshöfði heitir, ok skyldi þar hittast lið konungsins allt við höfðann.	This is with to get, that headland that went one side near the-sound, was Temple-Head named, and should there meet company the-king's all with headland.	It is now worth getting that the headland that went on one side near the sound was named Temple-Head and the king and his forces were all to meet at the headland.
En er Geirviðr konungr var albúinn, þá leiddi hann alþýðu til skips.	And when Geirvid the-king was all-ready, then led he the-people to the-ships.	But when King Geirvid was ready, he led the people to the ships.
Þar var í ferð með konungi Dagfinnr skáld.	There was on the-journey with the-king Dagfinn the-poet.	The poet Dagfinn was on the journey there with the king.
En í ofangöngunni til skipanna, þá varð sá atburðr, er geta verðr, þó at lítils vægis þykki vera, at losnaði skópvengr Dagfinns skálds.	But in over-going to the-ships, then was seen happening, which could worth, though that little weight thought being, that loosened shoe-thong Dagfinn's the-poet.	But in the passage to the ships, the event that can be mentioned, even though it is considered to be of little importance, was that the poet Dagfinn's shoelace came loose.
Ok síðan bindr hann þvenginn, ok þá vaknaði hann ok var þá Oddi, sem ván var, en eigi Dagfinnr.	And after tied he thong, and then woke he and was then Oddi, as expected was, and not Dagfinn.	And then he tied the shoelace, and then he awoke, and it was Odd, as was expected, but not Dagfinn.

The Tale of Star-Oddi's Dream (Old Norse)

Old Norse	Literal	English
Eftir þenna fyrirburð gekk Oddi út ok hugði at stjörnum, sem hann átti venju til jafnan, er hann sá út um nætr, þá er sjá mátti stjörnur.	After these visions went Oddi out and thought that the-stars, which he had habitually to always, that he saw out about night, then was saw might stars.	After these visions Oddi went out and thought about the stars which he had always seen many of at night.
Þá minntist hann á drauminn ok mundi allan nema kvæðit, þat er hann þóttist ort haf a í drauminum, nema þessar vísur sem hér eru ritnar:	Then remembered he the dream and thought everything except the-poem, that which he thought worded had so in the-dream, except this verse which here they-are written:	Then he remembered the dream and remembered everything except the poem he thought he had written in the dream except these verses written here:
Váru austr á Jöruskógi barmar tveir, böls of fylldir, ok til fjár fyrða næmdu við morðráð mörgu sinni.	They-were east in Battle-forest brothers two, spite about filled, and to wealth treasure took with murder many times.	There were in the east at Battle Forest two brothers filled with spite and for wealth they took treasure with murder many times.
En sá gramr, er gera bræðir, hefr tírgjarn tindótt hjarta, ok böðfrækn báða felldi Garp ok Gný Geirviðr konungr.	But that warrior, that made the-brothers, had fame-ambition toothed heart, and valiant both felled Garp and Gny Geirvid the-king.	But that anger that the brothers made had fame ambition with toothed heart and valiant felled both Garp and Gny King Geirvid.
Réð jafngjarn auði at skipta Róðbjarts sonr, rekka mærði af því fé, fyrða kindir, er svikmenni safnat höfðu.	Ruling equally riches to divide Hrodbjart's son, unfolded praise of for wealth, among-people kin, that the-wicked gathered had.	Ruling equally dividing the riches Hrodbjart's son, unfolded praise of that wealth among people and kinsmen that the wicked had collected.
Lét gunndjarfr gefna hringa seggja ætt siklingr Gauta, svát hirðmenn höfðu allir	Had the-treasurer given rings say descendants the-king Of-Goths, so-that court-men had all	the treasurer had given rings say descendants of the king of the Goths so that the court men had all

The Tale of Star-Oddi's Dream (Old Norse)

Old Norse	Literal	English
haukstóls hengiskafla.	hawk-seat mound-of-snow.	a hawk's seat on a mound of snow.
Mun Dagfinnr dýrra mála við lofsorð lúka kvæði. Njóti vel vegs ok landa gramr göfugr gauzkrar þjóðar.	Must Dagfinn dear words with praise conclude the-poem. Appreciate well glory and land warrior noble of-the-Goths king.	Dagfinn must with dear words and with praise conclude the poem. Enjoy well glory and land noble warrior king of the Goths.

8

En sem Oddi hafði úti verit slíka stund sem honum vel líkaði, fór hann inn í rekkju sína ok sofnaði þegar, ok dreymði hann þat sem it fyrra sinn ok hann hafði vaknat frá.	And as Oddi had out been such awhile as he well liked, fared he in to bed his and slept immediately, and dreamed he that which the first his and he had woken from.	But as Oddi had been outside for a moment which he liked well, he went into his bed and fell asleep at once, and dreamed it as the first time he had woken up from.
Þóttist hann þá hafa bundit skóþvenginn ok vera Dagfinnr ok skynda til skipanna.	Seemed to-him then had bound shoe-thong and was Dagfinn and hurrying to the-ships.	He then thought he had tied the shoelace and was Dagfinn and hurried to the ships.
Svá þótti honum í drauminum sem hann skyldi vera skipstjórnarmaðr.	So seemed to-him in the-dream as he should be ship-steering-man.	In his dream, he thought he was a captain.
Ok þegar þeir váru búnir til ferðar, fóru þeir með skipaflotann, til þess er þeir kómu við höfðann, ok hittist þar allt lið konungs, ok lögðu síðan fram í sundin Síldasund.	And as-soon-as they were ready to voyage, travel they with ship-fleet, to this that they came with headland, and met there all company the-king's, and laid then from to the-sound Herring-sound.	And when they were ready to go, they took the fleet until they came to the head, and there met all the king's army, and then put into the channel Herring-sound.
Þá er ok sagt, at þar var komin Hléguðr skjaldmær ok lá þar fyrir í sundunum með skipaflota sinn ok hafði ógrynni liðs ok albúin til orrostu.	Then is also said, that there was coming Hlegunn shield-maiden and lying there before the sound with ship-fleet hers and had mass company and all-prepared to battle.	It is also said that Hlegunn, a shield-bearer, had arrived there and lay there in the channels with her fleet of ships, and had an innumerable army ready for battle.

The Tale of Star-Oddi's Dream (Old Norse)

Old Norse	Literal	English
Síðan lögðu hvárir í mót öðrum, ok laust saman með þeim snarpri sókn, ok var þar inn harðasti bardagi, ok réðst brátt mikit mannfall í hvártveggja liði, en þó hafði eigi lengi staðit bardaginn, áðr en mannfallit hneig í lið konungs, ok hruðust hans skip mjök.	Afterwards laid each to meet each-other, and loosed together with they roughly attacked, and was there the hardest battle, and had soon much people-felled in each-way company, but though had none longer stood the-battle, before the people-felling strain to company the-king's, and cleared his ships much.	Then they put up a fight against each other, and a sharp attack broke out with them, and there was the hardest battle, and soon many casualties were inflicted on both sides, but the battle had not lasted long before the casualty fell to the king's army, and his ships were greatly wrecked.
Þess er ok getit, at Hléguðr varð ekki sén í orrostunni um daginn, ok hugðu menn þó drjúgt at af konungsmönnum, ok þótti þat undarligt.	It is also told-of, that Hlegunn was not seen in the-battle about the-day, and thought men though straight to of the-king's-men, and thought that wonder-like.	It is also mentioned that Hlegunn was not seen in the battle that day, and yet many of the king's men thought of it, and thought it strange.
En er slíku hafði fram farit langa hríð um daginn, þá leitaðist Dagfinnr um með sinni list, ok sá hann þá Hlégunni, ok var þá komin á konungsskipit, ok var þá orðin skipan mikil á hennar hag.	And when such had from gone long while about the-day, then sought Dagfinn about with his skills, and saw he then Hlegunn, and was then come to the-king's-ship, and was then become the-ship great about her circumstance.	But when such a thing had taken place for a long time that day, Dagfinn sought with his art, and he then saw Hlegunn, and had then come to the king's ship, and by then there had been a great order in her favour.
Honum sýndist á henni ylgjarhöfuð geysimikit ok tröllsligt ok biti með því höfuðin af konungsmönnum.	To-him seemed that her she-wolf's-head exceedingly-great and trollish and bit with against heads of the-king's-men.	It seemed to him that her head was a wolf's head, huge and trollish, and that it bit the heads of the king's men.
En er Dagfinnr sá þessi undr, þá steig hann af því skipi, er hann stýrði.	Then when Dagfinn saw this wonder, then leapt he off then the-ship, that he steered.	But when Dagfinn saw this miracle, he got off the ship he was steering.
Þat lá fjarri konungsskipinu.	It lay far-away the-king's-ship.	It was far from the king's ship.
Síðan hljóp hann hvert af öðru, unz hann kom á konungsskipit,	Afterwards ran he each of others, until he came to the-king's-ship,	Then he ran one by one until he came to the king's ship.
en þegar hann kom á fund konungs, þá sagði Dagfinnr, hvat títt var ok hvat stór endemi váru við.	then as-soon-as he came to find the-king, then said Dagfinn, what report was and that great unheard-of was against.	But when he came to meet the king, then Dagfinn said what was to report and what a great unheard of thing they were up against.

The Tale of Star-Oddi's Dream (Old Norse)

Old Norse	Literal	English
Síðan vísaði Dagfinnr konungi til, hvar Hléguðr var, at hann mætti sjá hana, en konungr fekk hana eigi sét sakir fjölkynngi hennar, en hitt sá hann, at menn hans féllu tugum saman.	Afterwards pointed-out Dagfinn the-king to, where Hlegunn was, that he may see her, but the-king got her not seen for-the-sake-of sorcery hers, but found saw he, that men his fell tens together.	Then Dagfinn referred to the king where Hlegunn was, that he might see her, but the king could not see her because of her witchcraft, but he saw that his men fell together by the dozens.
Þá bað Dagfinnr konunginn sjá undir hönd sér ina vinstri, ok svá gerði hann.	Then asked Dagfinn the-king look under hand his the left, and so did he.	Then King Dagfinn asked the king to see under his left hand, and so he did.
En er konungr fór svá með, þá sá hann Hlégunni.	And when the-king did so with, then saw he Hlegunn.	But when the king went with him, he saw Hlegunn.
Síðan gengu þeir báðir saman aftan til siglu.	Afterwards went they both together aft to sail.	Afterwards went they both together aft to sail.
Þá hljóp konungrinn fram með brugðnu sverði, ok þegar hann kemr í höggfæri við Hlégunni, þá höggr hann til hennar með sverðinu, ok kemr höggit á hálsinn, ok hjó hann af henni höfuðit, ok fell þat útbyrðis.	Then ran the-king forwards with drawn sword, and as-soon-as he came to striking-distance with Hlegunn, then struck he to her with sword, and came the-blow to neck, and hewed he off her head, and fell it overboard.	Then the king ran forward with a drawn sword, and when he came under attack with Hlegunn, he struck her with the sword, and the blow came on her neck, and he cut off her head, and it fell overboard.
En er hon var fallin, þá bauð konungrinn kost þeim mönnum, er fylgt höfðu Hlégunni, hvárt þeir vildi heldr halda bardaga upp við hann eða ganga honum til handa.	And when she was fallen, then offered the-king choice they the-people, who followed had Hlegunn, each they willed rather hold battle up with him or go him to hand.	But when she had fallen, the king offered the men who had followed Hlegunn whether they would rather fight him or go to his hand.
En þeir köru skjótt at ganga á konungs vald.	Then they chose quickly to go to the-king's power.	But they soon chose to enter into the king's power.
Ok síðan er Geirviðr lagði á braut ór þeim bardaga, þá lagði hann undir sik allt landit ok setr þar yfir sýslumenn ok friðaði svá allt ríkit.	And afterwards when Geirvid had to away from them the-battle, then had he under his all land and set there over stewards and peace so all the-kingdom.	And since King Geirviður set out from that battle, he conquered the whole country and placed it over the magistrates, and then pacified the whole kingdom.
Síðan helt konungr heim, ok var ger í mót honum dýrðlig veizla.	Afterwards held the-king home, and was made to meet him glorious feast.	Then the king returned home, and a glorious feast was held for him.
Eftir þat var kvatt þings, ok var þat þing allfjölmennt.	After it was summoned assembly, and was the assembly all-many-people.	After that an assembly was convened and that assembly was very crowded.

The Tale of Star-Oddi's Dream (Old Norse)

Old Norse	Literal	English
Var konungrinn Geirviðr settr þá enn á stól af nýju ok hafiðr upp á inn sama haug sem fyrr ok nú til konungs tekinn ok ríkisstjórnar yfir allt Gautland.	Was the-king Geirvid set then was on throne of new and raised up in the same mound as before and now to the-king taken and governor over all Götaland.	King Geirviður was then again put on a chair again and raised on the same mound as before and now taken to the king and the government over all of Götaland.
Gekk þá annarr höfðingi at öðrum upp á hauginn ok gerði til konungsins veg ok sóma, hverr eftir slíku, sem framast hafði föng ok færi á.	Went then one chieftain to another up to the-mound and made to the-king way and honour, each after such, as foremost had power and means of.	Then another chieftain went up to the hill, and made a way for the king, and honored each one according to all that he had.
Dagfinni skáldi kom þat í hug, at engi átti konunginum meiri virðing at launa í alla staði en hann.	Dagfinn the-poet came to the thought, that none had the-king more worthiness to repay in all places than him.	The poet Dagfinn thought that no one had more respect for the king in all respects than he.
Gekk hann síðan upp á hauginn ok kvaddi konunginn vel ok hæverskliga.	Went he then up on the-mound and greeted the-king well and modestly.	He then went up to the mound and greeted the king kindly and modestly.
Konungr tók glaðliga kveðju hans.	King took gladly greeting his.	The king gladly accepted his greeting.
Dagfinnr sagði konunginum deili á því, at hann hafði þá enn ort kvæði um hann af nýju, ok bað, at hann skyldi hlýða, ok kvaðst þá vilja færa kvæðit.	Dagfinn told the-king shared that accordingly, that he had then one worded a-poem about him of new, and asked, that he should listen, and spoke then willed bring the-poem.	Dagfinn told the king that he had written a poem about him again, and asked him to listen, and said he would bring the poem.
Konungrinn svarar, at hann kvaðst gjarna hlýða vilja.	The-king answered, that he said gladly listen willed.	The king replied that he will gladly listen.
Tók þá Dagfinnr ok flutti kvæðit, ok var þat þrítug drápa, er hann þóttist ort hafa.	Took then Dagfinn and brought the-poem, and was it thirty drapa, which he thought worded had.	Then Dagfinn took and recited the poem, and it was thirty stanza drapa which he thought he had written.

The Tale of Star-Oddi's Dream (Old Norse)

Old Norse	Literal	English
En er kvæðinu var lokit, þá þakkaði konungr þat allvel ok dró digran gullhring af hendi sér ok gaf Dagfinni at skáldskaparlaunum, en Dagfinnr vildi eigi þiggja hringinn ok sagðist allt ærit hafa, meðan hann heldi konunginum heilum,	And when the-poem was concluded, then thanked the-king it well and drew a-thick gold-ring of hand his and gave Dagfinn the poet's-reward, but Dagfinn willed not accept the-ring and said all abundance had, as-long-as he held the-king whole,	But when the poem was finished, the king thanked him very well and took a huge gold ring from his hand and gave Dagfinn a poet's reward, but Dagfinn did not want to accept the ring and said he had abundance as long as he kept the king whole.
en Geirviðr konungr lét þat þá í ljós við Dagfinn, at hann skyldi hans sóma meira gera í alla staði heldr en hvers manns annars í sínu ríki, ok bauð honum þat, at hann mundi afla honum kvánfangs, ok sagði svá, at hann mundi þá konu fá honum til handa, er hann vildi helzt kjósa náliga, þess er kostr var í því landi.	but Geirvid the-king had it then to light with Dagfinn, that he should him honour more do than all places rather than each man other in his kingdom, and offered him that, to him would gain him a-match, and said so, that he would then a-wife get him to hand, that he willed rather choose nearly, this as choice was in then the-land.	But King Geirvid then made it clear to Dagfinn that he should do him more honour in all respects than any other man in his kingdom, and offered him that he would give him a wife, and said that he would get a woman for him, which he preferred to choose, close by in the land whom Dagfinn most wanted to marry.
Dagfinnr tók þessu máli vel, sem ván var, er konungrinn vildi svá mikinn gera hans sóma, ok svarar:	Dagfinn took this matter well, as expected was, as the-king willed so much to-do him honour, and answered:	Dagfinn took this matter well, as was to be hoped, since the king wished so much to do him honour, and answered:
Ef þetta skal allt efna af yðvarri hendi við mik, sem nú er um mælt, þá er ekki því at leyna, at er sá kostrinn, at gjarna munda ek mér unna ok þú átt ok mest undir sjálfum þér",	If this shall all be-carried-out of your hand with me, as now is about spoken, then is not because that concealing, that is so choice, that gladly would I to-me love and you have and the-most under yourself to-you",	If all this is to be done by your hand with me, as is now said, then it is no secret that the choice is that I would gladly treat myself and you have and most of all under yourself.
Konungr mælti:	King spoke:	The king said,
Hver er sú kona, er þú talar til?"	Who is this woman, that you speak to?"	Who is the woman you are talking to?
Dagfinnr svarar:	Dagfinn answered:	Dagfinn answered:
Þat er Hlaðreið, systir þín.	It is Hladreid, sister yours.	It is Hladreid, your sister.
Hon er svá kvenna, at mér er mestr hugr á at fá, ella hygg ek, at fyrir muni farast um kvánföngin",	She is so the-woman, that to-me is the-greatest thinking that to marry, otherwise think I, that for should go about a-match",	She's so the woman that I'm most interested in marrying, otherwise I think about the match going".

The Tale of Star-Oddi's Dream (Old Norse)

Old Norse	Literal	English
Konungr sagði, at þat skyldi ok eigi undan draga við Dagfinn, er honum þótti sinn sómi vaxa við.	The-king said, that it should and not under drawn with Dagfinn, that he thought his honour grow with.	The king said that nothing should be denied to Dagfinn which he thought would increase his honour.
Hlaðreið konungssystir var þá gjafvaxta ok þó ung mjök at aldri, en kvenna var hon fegrst ok fríðust ok hezt at sér ger um alla hluti.	Hladreid the-king's-sister was then of-marriage-grown and though young much in age, but woman was she fairest and most-beautiful and the-best that herself made about all things.	Hlaðreið, the king's sister, was then gifted and yet very young, but of women she was the most fair and beautiful and the best at everything.
En hvárt sem þetta mál var talat lengr eðr skemr, þá ræðst þat af, að Hlaðreið var föstnuð Dagfinni skáldi.	And how as this matter was told longer or shorter, then decided it of, that Hladreid was betrothed-to Dagfinn the-poet.	But whether this matter was discussed longer or shorter, it was determined that Hladreid was engaged to the poet Dagfinn.
Síðan var þar fengit at boði, ok var þar ger in vegligasta veizla í alla staði með inum heztum tilföngum, því at ekki vantaði til, þat er hafa þurfti.	Afterwards was there got to announced, and was there done the greatest feast in all places with the best means, because that not lacking to, this was had need.	Then it was announced and there was the most successful feast in all respects with the best resources because there was no shortage of what was needed.
Þar var ok allt it hezta mannval, þat er í var landinu.	There were also all the best people, that were in were the-land.	There was also all the best selection of people in the country.
Var nú drukkit brúðhlaup þeira með inni mestu sæmð ok prýði.	Was now drunk the-wedding they with the most honour and finery.	Their wedding was now drunk with the greatest honour and splendor.
En er veizluna þraut, þá fór hverr til sinna heimkynna, er þangat hafði sótt.	And when the-feast finished, then travelled each to their households, that from-there had attended.	But when the feast ended, everyone who had gone there went to their own home.
En með þeim Dagfinni ok Hlaðreiði tókust brátt miklar ástir, ok var þeira samför einkar góð.	And between them Dagfinn and Hladreid took soon much love, and were they together very good.	And between Dagfinn and Hladreidi, they soon fell in love and their relationship was very good.
En er svá kurteisliga var komit ráðahag Dagfinns sem nú er frá sagt, þá var lokit drauminum, ok vaknaði hann þá, er Oddi var raunar.	But when so courtly was come marriage Dagfinn's as now was from said, then was ended the-dream, and awoke he then, that Oddi was actually.	But when in such a courtly fashion had Dagfinn's marriage taken place, as related, the dream ended, and he awoke that was actually Oddi.

The Tale of Star-Oddi's Dream (Old Norse)

Old Norse	Literal	English
# 9	# 9	# 9
Síðan hugði Oddi at um draum sinn ok mundi gersamliga drauminn allan, bæði inn fyrra ok svá inn síðara, ok minntist síðan á drápuna, þá er hann þóttist síðar kveðit hafa, ok mundi hann eigi fleira í kvæðinu heldr en þessar ellifu vísur, sem nú eru hér ritnar ok þetta er upphaf at:	Afterwards thought Oddi that about dream his and remembered completely the-dream all, both the first and so the latter, and remembered afterwards the drapa, then that he thought afterwards recited had, and would he not more of the-poem rather than these eleven verses, as now they-are here written and this is beginning of:	Then Odd thought of his dream and remembered the whole dream, both the first and then the second, and then remembered the drapa when he was thought to have recited later and he remembered no more in the poem than these eleven verses now written here and this is the beginning of:
Geirviðr of nam greiða gang, svát skreið ór þangi,	Geirvid of took ready going, so glided through seaweed,	Geirvid took ready going as gliding through seaweed
ok byrsóta beitti barð út of lágarða, ok seglhættu sóttu snarpir meðr ór veðri,	and windswept biting ship out about the-surf, and sail-danger attended sharply between with the-weather,	and windswept biting a ship out and about in the surf. and danger attended the sails sharp with the weather,
blés við hún, und Höfða,	blew with her, under Temple-Head,	blew against her under Temple Head,
harðan vegg of seggjum.	hard wall with men.	a hardened wall of men.
Skeið náði þá skríða	Sheathed-sword caught then action	The sheathed sword then caught ation
skjót of bylgjur ljótar. Fóru dyggir drengir á dýrmörum hlýra. Þar sák frægra fyrða för prúðligsta görva. Þó er gotneskra gumna Geirviðr konungr þeira.	launched about waves hideous. Travelled virtuous warriors in treasured bows. There saw famous fighters went most-prolific clearly. Yet of Gothic men Geirvid the-king theirs.	launched about hideous waves. Virtuous warriors travelled in treasured bows. There I saw famous fighters going most prolific and clearly. Yet of the Gothic men Geirvid is their king.
Sigldum Hofs fyrir höfða herðendr skipa ferðum göndul, grams, með landi,	We-sailed Temple before headland hardy the-ship's course Göndul, warriors, with land,	We sailed to Temple Head before the Headland hardy, the ship's course, Gondul, the warriors, with the land,
gótt ráð var þat dróttar, unz í Síldasundi sigrgöfgaðir vigrum hjuggu horskir seggir hjörs andskota börva.	good advice was that right, ours in Herring-sound victory-gift-gods spears striking brave said sword enemies trees.	good advice that was right, until in Herring-sound victorious god gifted spears striking bravely said the enemy sword trees.

The Tale of Star-Oddi's Dream (Old Norse)

Old Norse	Literal	English
Ok skjaldmeyja skjóma	And shield-maidens shimmering	And shield-maidens shimmering
skerðendr ok svá gerðu,	diminished and so doing,	did so diminish
at varfærir véar	with caution the-gods	with the caution of the gods
í vág fyrir lágu.	in inlet before laying-to.	in the inlet before laying-to.
Gátu ljónar líta	Could the-men see	The men could see
leiðangrs flota breiðan.	expedition fleet wide.	the expedition fleet wide.
Hilmis fór und hjálmi	Helmsman went under the-helm	The helmsman went under the helm,
hirð, sú er vörn of firrðisk.	court-men, so were defended over the-firth.	The court men, so were defended over the firth.
Brátt vöknuðu virðar	Soon awoke men	Soon awoke men
at vígboði þjóðar,	that battle-bidding great-river,	to the battle-bidding people
þá er Hlégunnar hestar	then were Hlegunn's horses	then were Hlegunn's horses
hafrastar mjök þustu	eagerly most flailing	eagerly most flailing
ok snarráðir sóttu	and quickly attended	and quickly attended
siklings vinir þingat.	the-king's friends assembled.	the king's friends assembled.
Þó er gotneskra gumna	Yet of Gothic men	And yet of all the Gothic men,
Geirviðr konungr þeira.	Geirvid king theirs.	Geirvid was their king.
Ok hnigsólar Högna	And stricken-sun Hogni's	And Hogni's stricken sun
hríð æxti þá síðan	awhile increased then after	increased awhile, then afterwards
blóðísunga beiðir,	blood-helmeted demanded,	the blood-helmeted demanded,
bragna konr, af magni,	heroes descended, of strength,	heroes descended, of strength,
en vígroða víða	then warfare wide	then warfare wide
varp af rómu snarpri.	thrown of battle rough.	thrown of battle rough.
Sjár varð dökkr af dreyra,	The-sea became dark of gore,	The sea became dark with gore
drótt þá er hríðmál sótti.	people then were storm encountered.	people then were storm encountered.
Svipun gerðisk þar sverða,	Swooping came there swords,	Swooping came there swords,
saman kómu þar rómu,	together came there a-roar,	together came there a-roar
göndul varð fyrir grundu,	Göndul became before ground,	Göndul fell to the ground,
grams drótt þvít vel sótti.	warriors right because well attended.	warriors right because that well attended.
Geirviðr of vá geiri,	Geirvid too guarded spears,	Geirvid too guarded spears,
geirvaldr, í hlökk þeiri.	spear-guardian, in looking-forward there.	spear-guardian in looking-forward there.
Blóðár sá ek í blóði.	Bloodied saw I in blood.	Bloodied, saw I in blood.
Blóð stökk of skor þjóða.	Blood leapt about across people.	Blood leapt about across the people.
Gerði hríð af hörðu	Made awhile of hordes	Made awhile of hordes

The Tale of Star-Oddi's Dream (Old Norse)

Old Norse	Literal	English
hirð sú, er fylkir stýrði.	court-men so, were commanded steered.	court-men so were commanding steered.
Margr er gramr af gengi göfugr tíginna jöfra. Spyrkat ek frægra fyrða ferð snjallari verða. Þó er gotneskra gumna Geirviðr konungr þeira.	Many were warriors of going noble high-born ruler. Learned I fame among-people journey most-valiant becomes. Though are Gothic men Geirvid the-king theirs.	Many were warriors of going noble high-born rulers. Learned I fame among-people journey most-valiant becomes. And yet of all the Gothic men, Geirvid was their king.
Hlégunnar leit ek hingat harðráðar ódáðir. Ýfð með ylgjar höfði eiskranlig réð geisa. Trölls kjafta sá ek tyggja tönnum hold af mönnum. Með hnitgeirum hváfta herða sókn of gerði.	Hlegunn sought I here hard-headed abhorrence. Bristling with wolf's head rage fixed furiously. Trolls jaws saw I chewing teeth the-bodies of men. With battle-spears wafting hard attack with done.	Hlegunn sought I here hard-headed abhorrence bristling with wolf's head rage fixed furiously. Troll's jaws saw I chewing teeth the-bodies of men. With battle-spears wafting a hard attack was done.
Annat sté ek af öðru Áta skíð of víði, unz glæsimar Gylfa gekk með hilmis rekkum,	One stepped I to another Stain wood about wood, until gleaming Gylfi went with the-helmsman upright,	I stepped from one to another stained wood about wood until gleaming Gylfi went with the helmsman upright
ok ek siklingi sagðak, sýslu ægis geisla hvé grimmhuguð gerði Gerðr of vígaferði.	and I the-king told, realm Aegir's gleam how grimly done Made too slayings.	and I told the king the realm of Aegir's gleam how grimly done made too slayings.
Gramr leit hitt, hvar hafði	Warrior sought to-meet, where had	The warrior sought to meet where had
Hörn hvergymis stjörnu höfuð á hauka stofni heiðingja sér brúðar. Ásynju lét elda örvígr konungr hníga flóðs af fyllar meiði frægr, hinn er ekki vægði.	Angled each star had upon hawk stem wolf her bride. The-goddesses had flames un-swinging the-king felled flood of full beam far-famed, that was no mercy.	each star anged had upon her hawk stem the wolf her bride. The Goddesses had flames unswinging the king felled flood of full beam far-famed, that was no mercy.
Nú er draum þessum lokit, er Stjörnu-Odda dreymði, eftir því sem hann sjálfr hefir sagt,	Now is the-dream this concluded, that Star-Oddi dreamed, after according as he himself has said,	Now this dream is over that Star-Oddi dreamed according to what he himself has said.

The Tale of Star-Oddi's Dream (Old Norse)

Old Norse	*Literal*	*English*
ok má víst undarligr ok fáheyrðr þykkja þessi fyrirburðr, en þó þykkir flestum líkligt, at hann muni þat eina sagt hafa, er honum hafi svá þótt verða í drauminum, því at Oddi var reiknaðr bæði fróðr ok sannsögull.	and may vision wonder-like and unusual seem this vision, but though seems most likely, that he would that only told have, what he had so thought happened in the-dream, because that Oddi was counted both wise and truthful.	And this phenomenon may be considered strange and unheard of, but most people still think that he will have said the only thing that seemed to him to be the case in the dream, because Oddur was considered both knowledgeable and truthful.
Má ok ekki undrast, þótt kveðskaprinn sé stirðr, því at í svefni var kveðit.	May also not wonder, thought poetry-making being stiff-footed, because that in sleep was recited.	It is not surprising that the poetry is stiff because it was recited in sleep.

Word List *(Old Norse to English)*

Old Norse	English
A, a	
a	so
að	that
aðra	other
aðrir	others
af	from, of, of, off, to
afla	gain
aflaði	obtained
afli	strength
aftan	aft
aftr	back, returning
albúin	all-prepared
albúinn	all-prepared, all-ready
albúnir	all-prepared
aldri	age, age, never, never
aldrigi	never
aldrs	of-age
aldrskominn	come-of-age
alla	all, all
allan	all, everything
allbráðliga	all-un-forethought
allfjölmennt	all-many-people
allir	all, all
allra	all, all
allráðligt	advisable
allri	all
alls	all
allt	all, all
allvel	well
alskipuð	fully-prepared
alþýðu	the-people
alvápnuðu	all-weaponed
andaðr	died
andast	died, died
andskota	enemies
annan	another, another
Annarr	one, one, the-other
annarrar	another
annars	anything-else, other, otherwise
annat	another, one
annathvárt	another-either, either-way
arminum	arm
at	a, in, it, of, so-as, that, the, then, to, with
atburð	events
atburðr	events, happening
atgervi	deeds
athæfi	behaviour
auðæfum	wealthy-treasures
auði	riches
aufúsa	gratitude
austr	east
Á, á	
á	about, at, by, in, of, on, that, the, then, to, upon
ábyrgð	responsibility
áðr	after, before
ágætum	wonderful
ágangi	aggression
áheyrsla	to-hear
ákafliga	extremely
ástir	love, love
ástúð	affection
ástvinum	beloved
Ásynju	the-goddesses
Áta	stain
átt	have, owned
átta	eight
átti	had
áttu	had
ávallt	always
áverka	injury
Æ, æ	
ægis	Aegir's (name)
ærit	abundance

Word List (Old Norse to English)

Old Norse	English
æsku	youth
ætla	intend
ætlat	intend
ætt	descendants, lineage
æxti	increased

B, b

Old Norse	English
bað	asked, invited
báða	both
báðir	both
báðu	asked
báðum	both
bæði	ask, both
bana	death
bar	bore, there
barð	ship
bardaga	battle, the-battle
bardagi	battle
bardaginn	the-battle
barmar	brothers
barn	child
barna	child
báru	brought
batnaði	bettering
bauð	offered
beðinn	asking
beiddi	asked
beiðir	demanded
beina	assistance
beitti	biting
bera	borne
berjast	battle, fight
berserkina	berserkers
berserkir	berserkers
berserkjanna	the-berserkers
berserkjunum	the-berserkers
betr	better
bezt	best
beztu	best
beztum	best
biðr	invited
bindr	tied
biti	bit
bjó	lived

Old Norse	English
blés	blew
blíðliga	joyfully
Blóð	blood
Blóðár	bloodied
blóði	blood
blóðísunga	blood-helmeted
böðfrækn	valiant
boði	announced
boðit	invited
böls	spite
borðum	the-tables
borin	brought
borit	bore, brought, carried
börva	trees
brá	drew
bræðir	the-brothers
bragna	heroes
brátt	soon
brattr	broad
braut	away
Bregðr	reaction
breið	broad
breiðan	wide
brott	away
brúðar	bride
brúðhlaup	the-wedding
brugðnu	drawn
brýtr	subduing
búa	prepare, prepared
búins	prepared
búit	preparations, prepared
bundit	bound
búnir	ready
burt	away
bylgjur	waves
byrjaði	began
byrsóta	windswept

D, d

Old Norse	English
Dagfinn	Dagfinn (name)
Dagfinni	Dagfinn (name)
Dagfinnr	Dagfinn (name)
Dagfinns	Dagfinn's (name)

Word List (Old Norse to English)

Old Norse	English
daginn	the-day
deili	shared
digran	a-thick
dökkr	dark
dóttur	a-daughter, daughter
draga	drawn
drápa	drapa
drápu	killed
drápuna	drapa
draum	dream, the-dream
drauminn	dream, the-dream
drauminum	the-dream
drengir	warriors
dreymði	dreamed
dreyra	gore
drjúgt	straight
dró	drew
drótt	people, right
dróttar	right
dróttning	the-queen
dróttningar	queen, the-queen
dróttningin	the-queen
drukkit	drank, drunk
drykk	drink
dvaldist	dwelled
dvelja	dwell
dyggir	virtuous
dýran	fine
dýrar	precious
dýrðlig	glorious
dyrigætti	doorway
dýrkuðu	adored
dýrmörum	treasured
dýrra	dear

E, e

Old Norse	English
eða	and, or
eðr	or
ef	if
efna	be-carried-out
eftir	after, afterwards
eiga	have, only
eigi	none, not
eiginkonu	wife
eignaði	owned
eigu	ownership
eina	only
einkar	very
einkum	especially, particularly
einn	one, only
eins	one
einsætt	evident
einum	one
eiskranlig	rage
eitt	one
eitthvert	some-time
ek	I
ekki	no, not
elda	flames
eldri	older
ella	either, or-else, otherwise
ellifu	eleven
elligar	otherwise
en	and, but, however, than, that, the, then, to, what, which
enda	and, with
endemi	unheard-of
engan	no
engi	no, none, not
enn	but, one, that, was
er	am, are, as, for, had, in, is, of, that, the, was, were, what, when, where, which, who
erendi	errand
erfð	honoured
erfi	a-toast
erfinu	the-toast
ert	are
Eru	are, they-are, was
eruð	are
eyjarinnar	the-island

F, f

Old Norse	English
fá	get, give, marry
faðir	father

Word List (Old Norse to English)

Old Norse	English
færa	bring
færi	journeyed, means, travel, went
fága	cultivate
fáheyrðr	unusual
fallin	fallen
fallinn	disposed
fallnir	fallen
fám	few
far	travel
fara	go, to-travel, travel, travelled
farandi	travel
farar	travel
fararinnar	of-the-journey
farast	go
farit	gone, travelling
farmóðr	travel-weary
fást	get
fátkaðist	few
fé	treasure, wealth
feðr	father
fegnir	celebrated
fegrst	fairest
féit	the-treasure
fekk	got
Félítill	fee-little
fell	fell
felldi	felled
fellu	fell
fengit	got
ferð	journey, the-journey
ferðar	journey, voyage
ferðina	travel, travelling
ferðinni	the-journey
ferðum	course
ferr	it-went, travelled
fertug	forty
firrðisk	the-firth
fiska	fishing
fjár	wealth
fjárins	wealth
fjarri	far-away
fjölkynngi	sorcery
fjölmenna	many-men
fjölmennan	followers-many
fjölmenni	followers, followers-many, many-followers
Flateyjar	Flatey (place)
fleira	more
flestum	most
flóðs	flood
flokkr	flokk
flota	fleet
flutti	brought
föður	father
fólki	folk
föng	possessions, power
fór	did, fared, travelled, went
för	journey, went
forkunnliga	exceedingly
fornum	ancient
fórst	travelled
fóru	going, travel, travelled, went
föruneyti	companionship
föstnuð	betrothed-to
Frá	from
frægð	fame
frægr	famous, far-famed
frægra	fame, famous
frændr	kinsmen
fráfall	death
fram	forwards, from
frama	fame
framast	foremost
frami	courage
frásaga	from-to-say
frásögu	from-saying
fremð	honour
friðaði	peace
fríðust	most-beautiful
fróðr	wise
fullgert	full-done
fullkomnir	fully-come
fullt	full
fullu	fully
fund	find, meet
fúsastr	willing
fylgð	follow
fylgi	follows

Word List (Old Norse to English)

Old Norse	English
fylgja	follow
fylgt	followed
fylkir	commanded
fyllar	full
fylldir	filled
fyrða	among-people, fighters, treasure
fyrir	because, before, for
fyrirburð	visions
fyrirburðr	vision
fyrr	before
fyrra	first
fyrst	first
fýstu	urged

G, g

Old Norse	English
gæfa	good-fortune
gæfu	luck
gaf	gave
gáfu	gave, have
gagn	won
gamall	old
gang	going
ganga	go, going
Garp	Garp (name)
Garpr	Garp (name)
gata	the-way
Gátu	could
Gauta	of-Goths
Gautland	Götaland (place)
Gautlandi	Götaland (place)
Gautlands	Götaland (place)
gauzkrar	of-the-Goths
gefa	give
gefna	given
geiri	spears
geirvaldr	spear-guardian
Geirvið	Geirvid (name)
Geirviðar	Geirvid (name)
Geirviði	Geirvid (name)
Geirviðr	Geirvid (name)
geisa	furiously
geisla	gleam
gekk	went
gengi	going
gengit	gone
gengr	went
gengu	went
ger	done, made
gera	be, do, made, to-do
gerði	did, done, made
gerðisk	came
gerðist	became, begins, happened
Gerðr	made
gerðu	doing, made
gerðust	made
gersamliga	completely
gert	done, made
gerzt	done
gestrinn	the-guest
geta	could, get
getit	told, told-of
geysimikit	exceedingly-great
gift	married
gistingar	guest
gjafvaxta	of-marriage-grown
gjarna	gladly
glaðliga	gladly
glæsimar	gleaming
glöggliga	clearly
Gný	Gny (name)
Gnýr	Gny (name)
góð	good
góðan	good
góðum	good
göfga	noble
göfugligum	noble-like
göfugr	noble
göndul	Göndul (place)
görva	clearly
gotneskra	Gothic (name)
gótt	good
götuna	path
grafinn	the-key
gramr	warrior, warriors
grams	warriors
greiða	ready
grimmhuguð	grimly
grundu	ground

Word List (Old Norse to English)

Old Norse	English
gullhring	a-gold-ring, gold-ring
gumna	men
gunndjarfr	the-treasurer
Gylfa	Gylfi (name)

H, h

Old Norse	English
hægliga	comfortable
hætta	conclude
hættliga	dangerously
hæverskliga	modestly
haf	had
hafa	had, have
hafði	had
hafi	had, have
hafiðr	raised
hafrastar	eagerly
haft	had
hag	circumstance
halda	hold
hálfs	half
hálsinn	neck
hamingjan	graciousness
hana	her, she
handa	hand, the-hand
handar	hand
Hann	he, him, it, to-him
hans	him, his, of-him
hár	high
harðan	hard
harðasti	hardest
harðfengi	toughness
harðráðar	hard-headed
harmaði	mourned
háska	danger
hátt	tall
háttar	kind
haug	a-mound, mound
hauginn	the-mound
hauginum	the-mound
hauka	hawk
haukstóls	hawk-seat
heðan	from-here
hefði	had, have
hefi	have

Old Norse	English
hefir	had, has, have
hefjast	start
hefr	had
heiðingja	wolf
heilum	whole
heim	home
heima	home
heiman	home
heimkynna	households
heimleiðis	homeward
heimt	drawn
heita	named
heitir	named
heitit	dominion
heldi	held
heldr	rather
Helgason	son-of-Helgi (name)
heljarmenn	accursed-men
helju	Hel (place)
helt	held
helzt	rather
hendi	hand
hengiskafla	mound-of-snow
hennar	her, hers
henni	her, hers, she, to-her
her	army
hér	forces, here, she
herða	hard
herðendr	hardy
herför	warfare
herjar	raided
herklæðum	war-clothes
herliði	war-company
hernað	raiding
hernaði	raiding
Herra	lord
hestar	horses
hét	named, was-named
heygðr	buried
heyrði	heard
heyrt	heard
hezt	the-best
hezta	best
heztum	best
Hildiguðr	Hildigunn (name)

40

Word List (Old Norse to English)

Old Norse	English
Hildigunnar	Hildigunn (name)
Hilmis	helmsman, the-helmsman
hina	then
hingat	here
hinn	that
hirð	court, court-men, retainers
hirðin	courtiers
hirðmaðr	court-man
hirðmenn	court-men
hirðmönnum	court-men
hitt	found, to-meet
hittast	meet
hittir	found
hittist	met
hjá	near
hjálmi	the-helm
hjarta	heart
hjó	hewed
Hjörguðr	Hjorgunn (name)
Hjörgunni	Hjorgunn (name)
hjörs	sword
Hjörvarðar	Hjorvard (name)
Hjörvarði	Hjorvard (name)
Hjörvarðr	Hjorvard (name)
hjuggu	striking
Hlaðreið	Hladreid (name)
Hlaðreiði	Hladreid (name)
Hléguðr	Hlegunn (name)
Hlégunnar	Hlegunn (name), Hlegunn's (name)
Hlégunni	Hlegunn (name)
hljóp	ran
hlökk	looking-forward
hlut	lot
hluta	things
hluti	things
hlutum	things
hlýða	listen, obey
hlýddi	followed
hlýra	bows
hneig	strain
hníga	felled
hnigsólar	stricken-sun
hnitgeirum	battle-spears
hóf	began
höfða	headland, Temple-Head (place)
höfðann	headland
höfði	head, headland
höfðingi	chieftain
höfðingja	a-chieftain, chieftains
höfðingjum	chieftains
höfðingliga	nobly
höfðu	had
Hofs	temple
Hofshöfði	Temple-Head (place)
hófu	had
höfuð	had
höfuðin	heads
höfuðit	head
högg	blows
höggfæri	striking-distance
höggit	the-blow
höggr	struck
hógligr	comfortably
Högna	Hogni's (name)
hold	the-bodies
hóli	hill
hólinn	the-hill
hólinum	the-hill
hóll	hill
hon	her, it, she
hönd	hand
honum	he, he, him, him, his, his, to-him
hörðu	hordes
Hörn	angled
horskir	brave
hræ	corpses
hríð	awhile, while
hríðmál	storm
hringa	rings
hringinn	the-ring
Hróðbjart	Hrodbjart (name)
Hróðbjarti	Hrodbjart (name)
Hróðbjartr	Hrodbjart (name)
Hróðbjarts	Hrodbjart's (name)
hruðust	cleared
hug	mind, thought
huga	minds

Word List (Old Norse to English)

Old Norse	English
hugði	thought
hugðu	thought
hugr	thinking
Hugsat	think
hulðu	covering
hún	her
hús	house
húsbóndi	housemaster
húsgerðar	house-builder
húsinu	the-house
húss	house
hváfta	wafting
hvar	where
hvárir	each
hvárki	neither
hvárt	each, either, how
hvártveggja	each-way
hvat	that, what
hvé	how
Hver	who
hvergi	each
hvergymis	each
hverjum	each
hverr	each, who
hverra	what
hvers	each
hversu	how-so
hvert	each
hygg	think

I, i

Old Norse	English
iðn	crafts
illvirki	outrages
illvirkjanna	for-the-evil-doers, the-evil-doers
illvirkjar	evil-doers
illvirkjarnir	criminals, the-evil-doers
illvirkjunum	evil-doers
in	the
ina	the
inn	in, the
innan	inside, within
inni	the
ins	the
inum	the, the-others
it	the

Í, í

Old Norse	English
í	about, at, in, of, on, than, the, to
Íslandi	Iceland (place)

J, j

Old Norse	English
jafnaldra	equal-age
jafnan	always
jafngjarn	equally
jarl	earl, the-earl
jarli	the-earl
jarls	the-earl
jarlsdóttir	the-earl's-daughter
játti	said
jöfra	ruler
Jöruskóg	Battle-forest (place)
Jöruskógi	Battle-forest (place)
Jöruskógr	Battle-forest (place)

K, k

Old Norse	English
kæmist	comes
kallaði	claimed
kallaðr	called
kann	can, known
kastaði	cast
kaupast	redeem
kaupferðir	merchant-voyages
kempum	champion
kemr	came
kindir	kin
kjafta	jaws
kjósa	choices, choose
kjósið	choose
kné	knee
kom	came
koma	came, come

Word List (Old Norse to English)

Old Norse	English
komin	come, coming
kominn	come
komir	come
komit	came, come
komnir	come, coming
kómu	came
kona	wife, wife-of, woman
konar	kinds-of
konr	descended
konu	a-wife, wife
konung	the-king
konungdóminn	kingdom
konungi	the-king
konunginn	the-king
konunginum	the-king
konungr	king, the-king
konungrinn	the-king, the-king's, this-king
konungs	king, the-king, the-king's
konungsins	the-king, the-king's
konungsmönnum	the-king's-men
konungsskáld	the-king's-poet
konungsskipinu	the-king's-ship
konungsskipit	the-king's-ship
konungssystir	the-king's-sister
konur	women
köru	chose
kost	choice
kostaboð	choice-bid
kostat	earned
kosti	benefits
kostir	choose
kostr	choice
kostrinn	choice, distinguished
kunna	know
kunnigt	know, known
kurteisliga	courtly
kvað	said, spoke
kvaddi	greeted
kvaðst	said, spoke
kváðu	said
kvæða	announced
kvæði	a-poem, the-poem
kvæðinn	poetry
kvæðinu	the-poem
kvæðit	the-poem
kvánfang	a-match
kvánfangs	a-match
kvánföngin	a-match
kvángaðr	married
kvatt	summoned
kveðit	recited
kveðja	called
kveðju	greeting
kveðskaprinn	poetry-making
kveldit	evening
kvenna	the-woman, woman
kvennasið	woman's-customs
kyns	kinds-of

L, l

Old Norse	English
lá	lay, lying
læst	locked
lágarða	the-surf
lagði	had
lagðist	lay
lagit	granted
lágu	laying-to
land	land
landa	land, lands
landi	land, the-land
landinu	the-land, the-land
landit	land
landráða	land-ruling
lands	lands, the-land, the-lands
landsfólkinu	lands-folk
landsfólkit	the-land's-people
landsmönnum	lands-people
landsstjórnin	the-government
landstjórnar	governing
langa	long
langar	long
langir	long
langskip	longships
langt	long
láta	allow, allowed, leave, let, lose, to-have
látast	die

Word List (Old Norse to English)

Old Norse	English
latti	discouraged
launa	repay, reward
laust	loosed
laut	place
leið	company, laid, passes, way
leiðangrs	expedition
leiddi	led
leiðir	led, took
leit	sought
leita	search, searching, seeking
leitaðist	sought
lengi	longer
lengr	longer
lengra	longer
lér	lean
lét	had
letja	discourage
letjast	discouraged
létu	had
létust	had
leyna	concealing
lið	company, crew
liði	company, crew
liðit	passed
liðs	company
liðskosti	provisions
líf	life
lifði	lived
lífi	alive
líflát	life-less
liggja	camped
líka	like
líkaði	liked
líkar	liked
líkligt	likely
list	skills
líta	look, see
lítil	little
lítill	little
lítils	little
litla	little
lítt	a-little, little
ljónar	the-men
ljós	light
ljósliga	lightly
ljótar	hideous
lofsorð	praise
lofuðu	praised
lögðu	laid
lögðust	camped, laid
lokit	concluded, ended
lönd	the-land
löng	long
losnaði	loosened
löttu	dissuaded
lúka	conclude
luku	unlocked
lygi	lied
lykðum	completion
lykill	buried
lykka	luck
lýsa	show

M, m

Old Norse	English
Má	may
maðr	a-man, man
mælt	spoke, spoken
mælti	spoke
mæltu	spoke
mærði	praise
mætti	may
magni	strength
maki	match
mál	matter
mála	words
máli	matter, saying, speech, the-matter
mann	man, man, person
mannaðir	mannered
mannaðr	brought-up
mannfall	people-felled
mannfallit	people-felling
manni	person
manns	man, man's
mannval	people
margir	many
Margr	many
margs	many

Word List (Old Norse to English)

Old Norse	English
Margt	many
mat	food
mátti	might
með	between, with
meðan	as-long-as, while
meðr	between
mega	may
megi	may
megin	side, sides
meiði	beam
mein	harm
meir	more
meira	more
meiri	more
menn	men, people
mér	for-me, me, to-me
merkiligsti	remarkable
mest	the-most
mesta	most
mesti	most
mestr	the-greatest
mestu	most
mik	me, myself
mikil	great, much
mikill	much
mikinn	great, much
mikit	great, greatly, much
mikla	much
miklar	much
miklir	great
miklu	great, much
miklum	much
millum	between
mína	my
minna	less
minnar	mine, my
minni	my
minntist	remembered
mínu	my
mínum	mine, my
missa	missed
misst	lost, missed
mitt	mine, my
mjök	most, much
móðir	mother
móður	mother
mönnum	men, people, the-people
morðráð	murder
mörg	many
morgininn	morning
mörgu	many
mörkinni	the-border
mót	meet
móti	meeting
móts	meet
Múla	Muli (place)
Mun	must, should
munda	would
mundi	may, remembered, thought, would
mundu	would
muni	should, would
munni	mouth

N, n

Old Norse	English
náði	caught
næðist	reached
næmdu	took
nær	near
næst	next
nætr	night
náliga	almost, closely, nearly
nam	took
nát	protection
né	nor
nefnd	named
nefndr	named
nema	except
Njóti	appreciate
nökkur	something, somewhat
nökkurr	someone
nökkurs	somewhat
nökkut	something, some-time, somewhat
norðr	in-the-north
nóttina	the-night
nú	how, no, now
nýju	new

Word List (Old Norse to English)

Old Norse	English

O, o

Old Norse	English
Odda	Oddi (name), Oddi's (name)
Oddi	Oddi (name)
of	about, of, over, too, with
ofan	over
ofangöngunni	over-going
oft	often
ok	also, and, of
orð	worded, words
orða	words
orðahjaldr	word-struggle
orðin	become
orðinn	become
orku	power
orrostu	battle
orrostunni	the-battle
ort	worded
oss	us

Ó, ó

Old Norse	English
óboðit	uninvited
ódáðir	abhorrence
ódælli	un-pleasant
ógrynni	mass
óhægendi	inconvenience
ójafnað	unequal
ójafnari	unequal
ólát	un-courteous
ór	from, out-of, through, with
ósnöfrmannliga	un-alert

Ö, ö

Old Norse	English
öðru	another, others
öðrum	another, each-other, to-other
ök	and
öllu	all
öllum	all, of-all
önnur	others
örvígr	un-swinging

P, p

Old Norse	English
presentur	presents
prúðligsta	most-prolific
prýði	finery

R, r

Old Norse	English
ráð	advice, decide, decision, statements
ráða	prevail
ráðahag	marriage, marriage-proposal
ráðast	arrange, arranging
ráði	conduct, consent, decision
ráðist	determine-to
ráðligt	advice
ráðvandr	honest
ræðst	decided
rammgert	firmly-built
raunar	actually
réð	fixed, ruled, ruling
réðst	had
réðust	appointed
reiknaðr	counted
rekka	unfolded
rekkju	bed
rekkum	upright
Reykjardal	Reykjardal (place)
reyna	test
riðu	rode
ríkar	rich
ríki	kingdom, the-kingdom
ríkinu	the-kingdom
ríkis	kingdom, the-kingdom
ríkisstjórnar	governor
ríkit	the-kingdom
ríkustum	kingdom's
rímkænn	calendar-computation-wise

Word List (Old Norse to English)

Old Norse	English
ritnar	written
rjóðr	clearing
Róðbjarts	Hrodbjart's (name)
rómu	a-roar, battle

S, s

Old Norse	English
sá	saw, seen, so, that
sæi	saw
sækja	seek, sought
sæma	honour, the-same
sæmð	honour
sæmði	honour
sæmiligar	honourable
safnar	gathered
safnat	gathered
sagan	the-saga
sagðak	told
sagði	said, telling, the-saga, told, told
sagðist	said
sagt	said, said, told
sák	saw
sakir	for-the-sake-of, sake, the-sake-of
sama	same
saman	the-same, together
sameignar	fight, the-fight
samfarar	interaction
samför	together, togetherness
samtíða	contemporary
sannsögull	truthful
sárum	wounds
sat	sat
satt	the-truth
sé	are, being
seggir	said
seggja	say
seggjum	men
segir	said
segja	said, say
seglhættu	sail-danger
seldr	sold
sem	as, so, that, was, which
sén	seen
sendi	sent
sendimenn	messengers, sending-men
sendir	sent
sér	are, as, he, her, herself, himself, his, themselves
sét	seen
setr	set
sett	sat, set
settan	appointed
setti	set
settr	sat, set
sið	traditions
síðan	after, afterwards, then
síðar	afterwards
síðara	latter
Sigldum	we-sailed
siglu	sail
sigr	victory
sigrgöfgaðir	victory-gift-gods
sigri	victory
sik	herself, himself, his, themselves
siklingi	the-king
siklingr	the-king
siklings	the-king's
Síldasund	Herring-sound (place)
Síldasundi	Herring-sound (place)
sín	her, his, their
sína	himself, his
sinn	her, hers, his, one-day
sinna	their
sinni	hers, his, times
síns	his
sínu	her, his
sínum	hers, theirs
sitja	sit
sitt	his, their
sjá	look, saw, see, so
sjáir	look
sjálf	herself

Word List (Old Norse to English)

Old Norse	English	Old Norse	English
sjálfr	himself	*skóginn*	the-forest
sjálfum	himself, yourself	*skor*	across
Sjár	the-sea	*skorta*	shortage
sjást	t-look	*skorti*	shortage
skaði	harm	*skóþvenginn*	shoe-thong
skafti	spear	*skóþvengr*	shoe-thong
skal	shall	*skreið*	glided
skáld	poet, the-poet	*skríða*	action
skáldi	the-poet	*skuluð*	should
skáldinu	the-poet	*skyldari*	obliged
skálds	the-poet	*skyldi*	should
skáldskaparlaunum	poet's-reward	*skynda*	hurrying
Skeið	sheathed-sword	*slíka*	such
skemmtanar	entertainment	*slíks*	such
skemr	shorter	*Slíku*	so, such
skerðendr	diminished	*slíkum*	such
skíð	wood	*smágrjót*	small-stones
skildi	shield	*snarpir*	sharply
skilði	should	*snarpri*	rough, roughly
skilðu	knew	*snarráðir*	quickly
skiljast	separate	*snemma*	soon
skilnaðr	parting	*snjallari*	most-valiant
skip	ships	*snýr*	turned
skipa	the-ship's	*sofnaði*	slept
skipaflota	ship-fleet	*sofnar*	slept
skipaflotann	ship-fleet	*sögðu*	said
skipan	the-ship	*sögu*	telling
skipanna	the-ships	*söguna*	the-saga
skipi	the-ship	*sögunnar*	the-saga
skips	the-ships	*sögunni*	the-saga
skipstjórnarmaðr	ship-steering-man	*sókn*	attack, attacked
skipta	divide, exchange	*sóma*	honour
skipti	exchanged	*sómasamligri*	respectable
skiptum	exchanged	*sómi*	honour
skipuð	prepared	*son*	son
skjaldmær	shield-maiden	*sonar*	son
skjaldmeyja	shield-maidens	*sonr*	son
skjaldmeyjar	shield-maidens	*sótt*	attended, sickness
skjóma	shimmering	*sótti*	attended, attending, encountered
skjót	launched		
skjóta	short, throw	*sóttin*	sickness
skjótara	shorter	*sóttu*	attended
skjótast	quickly, soonest	*spurði*	asked
skjótt	quickly	*spyrjast*	was-heard
skóg	forest	*Spyrkat*	learned
		stað	place

48

Word List (Old Norse to English)

Old Norse	English
staddir	standing
staddr	placed, stood
staði	places
staðit	placed, stood
standa	standing
sté	stepped
steig	leapt
sterkr	strong
stíg	path
stigamannanna	the-robbing-men
stigamönnum	the-robbers
stígr	climbed
stirðr	stiff-footed
stjórn	control
stjórna	ruling
stjörnu	star
stjörnum	the-stars
Stjörnu-Odda	Star-Oddi (name)
Stjörnu-Oddi	Star-Oddi (name)
stjörnur	stars
stóð	place, stood
stóðu	stood
stofnat	planned
stofni	stem
stökk	leapt
stól	throne
stór	great
stóra	great
stórmannliga	great-man-like
stórum	great
stund	awhile
stýrði	guided, steered
Sú	so, this
Sumir	some
sund	a-sound
sundin	the-sound
sundunum	sound, the-sound
svá	so, such, to
svarar	answer, answered
svari	answer
svát	so, so-that
svefni	sleep
sverða	swords
sverði	sword
sverðinu	sword
svikmenni	the-wicked
Svipun	swooping
svívirðing	disgraceful
sýndist	seemed
sýnist	seems
sýslu	realm
sýslumenn	stewards
systir	sister

T, t

Old Norse	English
taka	take, taken
takast	take, took
talar	speak
talat	told
talði	said
tekinn	taken
tekr	took
tekst	takes
tíðenda	news
tíðendi	news, the-news
tíðendin	news
tíðendum	news
tíginna	high-born
tígn	prestige
tígnar	princely
til	for, that, to
tilföngum	means
tíma	time
tímar	time
tindótt	toothed
tírgjarn	fame-ambition
títt	report
tízka	fashion
tját	expressed
tjóa	avail
tók	took
tókust	took
tölðu	told
tólf	twelve
tönnum	teeth
treysta	trust
Trölls	trolls
tröllsligt	trollish
tryggðarmaðr	faithful-man

Word List (Old Norse to English)

Old Norse	English
tugum	tens
tvá	two
tveggja	two
tveir	two
tyggja	chewing

Þ, þ

Old Norse	English
þá	then
Þaðan	from-there, then
Þær	they
þætti	seemed, thought
þakkaði	thanked
þakkar	thanked
þangat	from-there, there
þangi	seaweed
þann	that, then
þar	of, that, then, there, they
þarf	needed
þat	it, that, the, then, they, this, to
þau	the, there, they
þegar	as-soon-as, immediately, straightaway, they
þegnum	subjects
þeim	them, they
þeir	them, there, they
þeira	of-them, their, theirs, them, there, they
þeiri	that, there
þenna	these, this
þér	to-you, you
Þess	it, the, this
þessa	of-this, these, this
þessar	these, this
þessarar	this
þessari	this
þessi	the, these, this
Þessir	these
þessu	this
þessum	this
þetta	that, the, this
þiggja	accept
þik	you
þín	yours
þing	assembly, the-assembly
þingat	assembled
þings	an-assembly, assembly
þjóða	people
þjóðar	great-river, king
þjóðbrautinni	the-highway
þó	though, yet
Þórðr	Thord (name)
þótt	though, thought
þótti	seemed, thought
Þóttist	seemed, though, thought
þóttust	thought
þraut	finished
þrekvirki	brave-deeds
þriðjung	a-third-of
þrítug	thirty
þrjú	three
þroskast	develop
þú	you
þurfa	needed
þurfti	need
þustu	flailing
þvenginn	thong
því	according, accordingly, according-to, against, because, for, then, therefore
þvílíks	such-like
þvít	because
þykki	thought
þykkir	seemed, seems
þykkja	regarded, seem

U, u

Old Norse	English
um	about
umbúnaðr	soft-bed-prepared
ummæli	about-words
umsjá	supervision
und	under

Word List (Old Norse to English)

Old Norse	English
undan	under
undarligr	extraordinary, wonder-like
undarligt	wonder-like
undir	under
undr	wonder
undrast	wonder
ung	young
unga	young
ungr	young
unna	grant, love
unz	ours, until
upp	up
upphaf	beginning
upphafi	became
uppheldi	advancement
urðu	became

Ú, ú

Old Norse	English
út	out, out-from
útan	without
útbyrðis	overboard
úti	out
útilegumannanna	the-outlaw-men

V, v

Old Norse	English
vá	guarded
vægði	mercy
vægis	weight
vænn	handsome
væri	being, was, were, would-be
vág	inlet
vaknaði	awoke, woke
vaknat	woken
vakni	wake
vald	power
valda	wield
ván	expected, expecting
vandræði	difficulty
vanir	friends
vanr	accustomed

Old Norse	English
vantaði	lacking
vápnaðir	weaponed
vápnaskipti	weapons-exchange
vápnfimi	weapon-nimble
vápnum	weapons
var	was, were
vár	our
varð	became, was
varfærir	caution
varp	thrown
várr	our
várrar	aware
Váru	they-were, was, were
vaxa	grow
vaxit	grown
véar	the-gods
veðri	the-weather
veg	way
vega	ways
vegg	wall
vegligasta	greatest
vegs	glory
veit	know
veitt	given
veitti	gave
veittr	given
veizla	feast
veizlu	feast
veizluna	feast, the-feast
veizlunni	the-feast
vel	all, well
velja	choose
venja	way
venju	habitually
vera	be, being, was
verða	be, become, becomes, happened, to-be, worthy
verði	be
verðr	became, worth
verit	been
verkmaðr	working-man
vetra	winters
vexti	grown
við	against, trees, with
víða	wide, widely, with

Word List (Old Norse to English)

Old Norse	English
viðbúnaði	preparation
víði	wood
vígaferði	slayings
vígboði	battle-bidding
vígroða	warfare
vigrum	spears
víking	viking, viking-raids
víkinga	vikings
víkingar	vikings
vil	will, wish
vildi	willed, wished
vildu	willed, wished
vili	wish
vilið	wish
vilja	willed
vill	wanted-to, will, wish
villtu	will-you
vinir	friends
vinna	grant
vinstri	left
vinum	friends
virðar	men
virðing	worth, worthiness, worthy
virðingu	worthiness
virðuliga	worthily
virðuligr	worthy
virðuligri	worthy
virkðamönnum	chosen-man
virkðavinum	friends
vísaði	pointed-out
viss	aware
vissi	knew
vissir	know
vist	hospitality
víst	vision
vísur	verse, verses
vit	to
vita	knew, know, to-know
vitja	visit
vitmikill	knowing-much
vitr	wise
vitrasta	wisest
vitrustum	wise
vöknuðu	awoke
vörn	defended

Y, y

Old Norse	English
yðr	of-you, to-you, you
yðvarrar	your
yðvarri	your
yfir	over
yfirkoma	overcome
ylgjar	wolf's
ylgjarhöfuð	she-wolf's-head
yrði	became

Ý, ý

Old Norse	English
Ýfð	bristling
ýmissa	various

Word List *(English to Old Norse)*

English	Old Norse

A, a

English	Old Norse
a	at
abhorrence	ódáðir
about	á, í, of, um
about-words	ummæli
abundance	ærit
accept	þiggja
according	því
accordingly	því
according-to	því
accursed-men	heljarmenn
accustomed	vanr
a-chieftain	höfðingja
across	skor
action	skríða
actually	raunar
a-daughter	dóttur
adored	dýrkuðu
advancement	uppheldi
advice	ráð, ráðligt
advisable	allráðligt
Aegir's (name)	ægis
affection	ástúð
aft	aftan
after	áðr, eftir, síðan
afterwards	eftir, síðan, síðar
against	því, við
age	aldri
aggression	ágangi
a-gold-ring	gullhring
a-little	lítt
alive	lífi
all	alla, allan, allir, allra, allri, alls, allt, öllu, öllum, vel
all-many-people	allfjölmennt
allow	láta
allowed	láta
all-prepared	albúin, albúinn, albúnir
all-ready	albúinn
all-un-forethought	allbráðliga
all-weaponed	alvápnuðu
almost	náliga
also	ok
always	ávallt, jafnan
am	er
a-man	maðr
a-match	kvánfang, kvánfangs, kvánföngin
among-people	fyrða
a-mound	haug
an-assembly	þings
ancient	fornum
and	eða, en, enda, ok, ök
angled	Hörn
announced	boði, kvæða
another	annan, annarrar, annat, öðru, öðrum
another-either	annathvárt
answer	svarar, svari
answered	svarar
anything-else	annars
a-poem	kvæði
appointed	réðust, settan
appreciate	Njóti
are	er, ert, Eru, eruð, sé, sér
arm	arminum
army	her
a-roar	rómu
arrange	ráðast
arranging	ráðast
as	er, sem, sér
ask	bæði
asked	bað, báðu, beiddi, spurði
asking	beðinn
as-long-as	meðan
a-sound	sund
assembled	þingat
assembly	þing, þings
assistance	beina
as-soon-as	þegar

Word List (English to Old Norse)

English	Old Norse
at	á, í
a-thick	digran
a-third-of	þriðjung
a-toast	erfi
attack	sókn
attacked	sókn
attended	sótt, sótti, sóttu
attending	sótti
avail	tjóa
aware	várrar, viss
away	braut, brott, burt
awhile	hríð, stund
a-wife	konu
awoke	vaknaði, vöknuðu

B, b

English	Old Norse
back	aftr
battle	bardaga, bardagi, berjast, orrostu, rómu
battle-bidding	vígboði
Battle-forest (place)	Jöruskóg, Jöruskógi, Jöruskógr
battle-spears	hnitgeirum
be	gera, vera, verða, verði
beam	meiði
became	gerðist, upphafi, urðu, varð, verðr, yrði
be-carried-out	efna
because	fyrir, því, þvít
become	orðin, orðinn, verða
becomes	verða
bed	rekkju
been	verit
before	áðr, fyrir, fyrr
began	byrjaði, hóf
beginning	upphaf
begins	gerðist
behaviour	athæfi
being	sé, væri, vera
beloved	ástvinum
benefits	kosti
berserkers	berserkina, berserkir
best	bezt, beztu, beztum, hezta, heztum
betrothed-to	föstnuð
better	betr
bettering	batnaði
between	með, meðr, millum
bit	biti
biting	beitti
blew	blés
blood	Blóð, blóði
blood-helmeted	blóðísunga
bloodied	Blóðár
blows	högg
bore	bar, borit
borne	bera
both	báða, báðir, báðum, bæði
bound	bundit
bows	hlýra
brave	horskir
brave-deeds	þrekvirki
bride	brúðar
bring	færa
bristling	Ýfð
broad	brattr, breið
brothers	barmar
brought	báru, borin, borit, flutti
brought-up	mannaðr
buried	heygðr, lykill
but	en, enn
by	á

C, c

English	Old Norse
calendar-computation-wise	rímkænn
called	kallaðr, kveðja
came	gerðisk, kemr, kom, koma, komit, kómu
camped	liggja, lögðust
can	kann
carried	borit
cast	kastaði
caught	náði
caution	varfærir
celebrated	fegnir
champion	kempum

Word List (English to Old Norse)

English	Old Norse
chewing	tyggja
chieftain	höfðingi
chieftains	höfðingja, höfðingjum
child	barn, barna
choice	kost, kostr, kostrinn
choice-bid	kostaboð
choices	kjósa
choose	kjósa, kjósið, kostir, velja
chose	köru
chosen-man	virkðamönnum
circumstance	hag
claimed	kallaði
cleared	hruðust
clearing	rjóðr
clearly	glöggliga, görva
climbed	stígr
closely	náliga
come	koma, komin, kominn, komir, komit, komnir
come-of-age	aldrskominn
comes	kæmist
comfortable	hægliga
comfortably	hógligr
coming	komin, komnir
commanded	fylkir
companionship	föruneyti
company	leið, lið, liði, liðs
completely	gersamliga
completion	lykðum
concealing	leyna
conclude	hætta, lúka
concluded	lokit
conduct	ráði
consent	ráði
contemporary	samtíða
control	stjórn
corpses	hræ
could	Gátu, geta
counted	reiknaðr
courage	frami
course	ferðum
court	hirð
courtiers	hirðin
courtly	kurteisliga
court-man	hirðmaðr
court-men	hirð, hirðmenn, hirðmönnum
covering	hulðu
crafts	iðn
crew	lið, liði
criminals	illvirkjarnir
cultivate	fága

D, d

English	Old Norse
Dagfinn (name)	Dagfinn, Dagfinni, Dagfinnr
Dagfinn's (name)	Dagfinns
danger	háska
dangerously	hættliga
dark	dökkr
daughter	dóttur
dear	dýrra
death	bana, fráfall
decide	ráð
decided	ræðst
decision	ráð, ráði
deeds	atgervi
defended	vörn
demanded	beiðir
descendants	ætt
descended	konr
determine-to	ráðist
develop	þroskast
did	fór, gerði
die	látast
died	andaðr, andast
difficulty	vandræði
diminished	skerðendr
discourage	letja
discouraged	latti, letjast
disgraceful	svívirðing
disposed	fallinn
dissuaded	löttu
distinguished	kostrinn
divide	skipta
do	gera
doing	gerðu
dominion	heitit
done	ger, gerði, gert, gerzt

Word List (English to Old Norse)

English	Old Norse
doorway	dyrigætti
drank	drukkit
drapa	drápa, drápuna
drawn	brugðnu, draga, heimt
dream	draum, drauminn
dreamed	dreymði
drew	brá, dró
drink	drykk
drunk	drukkit
dwell	dvelja
dwelled	dvaldist

E, e

English	Old Norse
each	hvárir, hvárt, hvergi, hvergymis, hverjum, hverr, hvers, hvert
each-other	öðrum
each-way	hvártveggja
eagerly	hafrastar
earl	jarl
earned	kostat
east	austr
eight	átta
either	ella, hvárt
either-way	annathvárt
eleven	ellifu
encountered	sótti
ended	lokit
enemies	andskota
entertainment	skemmtanar
equal-age	jafnaldra
equally	jafngjarn
errand	erendi
especially	einkum
evening	kveldit
events	atburð, atburðr
everything	allan
evident	einsætt
evil-doers	illvirkjar, illvirkjunum
exceedingly	forkunnliga
exceedingly-great	geysimikit
except	nema
exchange	skipta
exchanged	skipti, skiptum
expected	ván
expecting	ván
expedition	leiðangrs
expressed	tját
extraordinary	undarligr
extremely	ákafliga

F, f

English	Old Norse
fairest	fegrst
faithful-man	tryggðarmaðr
fallen	fallin, fallnir
fame	frægð, frægra, frama
fame-ambition	tírgjarn
famous	frægr, frægra
far-away	fjarri
fared	fór
far-famed	frægr
fashion	tízka
father	faðir, feðr, föður
feast	veizla, veizlu, veizluna
fee-little	Félítill
fell	fell, fellu
felled	felldi, hníga
few	fám, fátkaðist
fight	berjast, sameignar
fighters	fyrða
filled	fylldir
find	fund
fine	dýran
finery	prýði
finished	þraut
firmly-built	rammgert
first	fyrra, fyrst
fishing	fiska
fixed	réð
flailing	þustu
flames	elda
Flatey (place)	Flateyjar
fleet	flota
flokk	flokkr
flood	flóðs
folk	fólki
follow	fylgð, fylgja

Word List (English to Old Norse)

English	Old Norse
followed	fylgt, hlýddi
followers	fjölmenni
followers-many	fjölmennan, fjölmenni
follows	fylgi
food	mat
for	er, fyrir, því, til
forces	hér
foremost	framast
forest	skóg
for-me	mér
for-the-evil-doers	illvirkjanna
for-the-sake-of	sakir
forty	fertug
forwards	fram
found	hitt, hittir
friends	vanir, vinir, vinum, virkðavinum
from	af, Frá, fram, ór
from-here	heðan
from-saying	frásögu
from-there	Þaðan, þangat
from-to-say	frásaga
full	fullt, fyllar
full-done	fullgert
fully	fullu
fully-come	fullkomnir
fully-prepared	alskipuð
furiously	geisa

G, g

English	Old Norse
gain	afla
Garp (name)	Garp, Garpr
gathered	safnar, safnat
gave	gaf, gáfu, veitti
Geirvid (name)	Geirvið, Geirviðar, Geirviði, Geirviðr
get	fá, fást, geta
give	fá, gefa
given	gefna, veitt, veittr
gladly	gjarna, glaðliga
gleam	geisla
gleaming	glæsimar
glided	skreið
glorious	dýrðlig
glory	vegs
Gny (name)	Gný, Gnýr
go	fara, farast, ganga
going	fóru, gang, ganga, gengi
gold-ring	gullhring
Göndul (place)	göndul
gone	farit, gengit
good	góð, góðan, góðum, gótt
good-fortune	gæfa
gore	dreyra
got	fekk, fengit
Götaland (place)	Gautland, Gautlandi, Gautlands
Gothic (name)	gotneskra
governing	landstjórnar
governor	ríkisstjórnar
graciousness	hamingjan
grant	unna, vinna
granted	lagit
gratitude	aufúsa
great	mikil, mikinn, mikit, miklir, miklu, stór, stóra, stórum
greatest	vegligasta
greatly	mikit
great-man-like	stórmannliga
great-river	þjóðar
greeted	kvaddi
greeting	kveðju
grimly	grimmhuguð
ground	grundu
grow	vaxa
grown	vaxit, vexti
guarded	vá
guest	gistingar
guided	stýrði
Gylfi (name)	Gylfa

H, h

English	Old Norse
habitually	venju

Word List (English to Old Norse)

English	Old Norse
had	átti, áttu, er, haf, hafa, hafði, hafi, haft, hefði, hefir, hefr, höfðu, hófu, höfuð, lagði, lét, létu, létust, réðst
half	hálfs
hand	handa, handar, hendi, hönd
handsome	vænn
happened	gerðist, verða
happening	atburðr
hard	harðan, herða
hardest	harðasti
hard-headed	harðráðar
hardy	herðendr
harm	mein, skaði
has	hefir
have	átt, eiga, gáfu, hafa, hafi, hefði, hefi, hefir
hawk	hauka
hawk-seat	haukstóls
he	Hann, honum, sér
head	höfði, höfuðit
headland	höfða, höfðann, höfði
heads	höfuðin
heard	heyrði, heyrt
heart	hjarta
Hel (place)	helju
held	heldi, helt
helmsman	Hilmis
her	hana, hennar, henni, hon, hún, sér, sín, sinn, sínu
here	hér, hingat
heroes	bragna
Herring-sound (place)	Síldasund, Síldasundi
hers	hennar, henni, sinn, sinni, sínum
herself	sér, sik, sjálf
hewed	hjó
hideous	ljótar
high	hár
high-born	tíginna
Hildigunn (name)	Hildiguðr, Hildigunnar
hill	hóli, hóll
him	hann, hans, honum
himself	sér, sik, sína, sjálfr, sjálfum
his	hans, honum, sér, sik, sín, sína, sinn, sinni, síns, sínu, sitt
Hjorgunn (name)	Hjörguðr, Hjörgunni
Hjorvard (name)	Hjörvarðar, Hjörvarði, Hjörvarðr
Hladreid (name)	Hlaðreið, Hlaðreiði
Hlegunn (name)	Hléguðr, Hlégunnar, Hlégunni
Hlegunn's (name)	Hlégunnar
Hogni's (name)	Högna
hold	halda
home	heim, heima, heiman
homeward	heimleiðis
honest	ráðvandr
honour	fremð, sæma, sæmð, sæmði, sóma, sómi
honourable	sæmiligar
honoured	erfð
hordes	hörðu
horses	hestar
hospitality	vist
house	hús, húss
house-builder	húsgerðar
households	heimkynna
housemaster	húsbóndi
how	hvárt, hvé, nú
however	En
how-so	hversu
Hrodbjart (name)	Hróðbjart, Hróðbjarti, Hróðbjartr
Hrodbjart's (name)	Hróðbjarts, Róðbjarts
hurrying	skynda

I, i

English	Old Norse
I	ek
Iceland (place)	Íslandi
if	ef
immediately	þegar
in	á, at, er, í, inn
inconvenience	óhægendi
increased	æxti
injury	áverka

Word List (English to Old Norse)

English	Old Norse
inlet	vág
inside	innan
intend	ætla, ætlat
interaction	samfarar
in-the-north	norðr
invited	bað, biðr, boðit
is	er
it	at, Hann, hon, þat, Þess
it-went	ferr

J, j

English	Old Norse
jaws	kjafta
journey	ferð, ferðar, för
journeyed	færi
joyfully	blíðliga

K, k

English	Old Norse
killed	drápu
kin	kindir
kind	háttar
kinds-of	konar, kyns
king	konungr, konungs, þjóðar
kingdom	konungdóminn, ríki, ríkis
kingdom's	ríkustum
kinsmen	frændr
knee	kné
knew	skilðu, vissi, vita
know	kunna, kunnigt, veit, vissir, vita
knowing-much	vitmikill
known	kann, kunnigt

L, l

English	Old Norse
lacking	vantaði
laid	leið, lögðu, lögðust
land	land, landa, landi, landit
land-ruling	landráða
lands	landa, lands
lands-folk	landsfólkinu
lands-people	landsmönnum
latter	síðara
launched	skjót
lay	lá, lagðist
laying-to	lágu
lean	lér
leapt	steig, stökk
learned	Spyrkat
leave	láta
led	leiddi, leiðir
left	vinstri
less	minna
let	láta
lied	lygi
life	líf
life-less	líflát
light	ljós
lightly	ljósliga
like	líka
liked	líkaði, líkar
likely	líkligt
lineage	ætt
listen	hlýða
little	lítil, lítill, lítils, litla, lítt
lived	bjó, lifði
locked	læst
long	langa, langar, langir, langt, löng
longer	lengi, lengr, lengra
longships	langskip
look	líta, sjá, sjáir
looking-forward	hlökk
loosed	laust
loosened	losnaði
lord	Herra
lose	láta
lost	misst
lot	hlut
love	ástir, unna
luck	gæfu, lykka
lying	lá

Word List (English to Old Norse)

English	Old Norse

M, m

English	Old Norse
made	ger, gera, gerði, Gerðr, gerðu, gerðust, gert
man	maðr, mann, manns
mannered	mannaðir
man's	manns
many	margir, Margr, margs, Margt, mörg, mörgu
many-followers	fjölmenni
many-men	fjölmenna
marriage	ráðahag
marriage-proposal	ráðahag
married	gift, kvángaðr
marry	fá
mass	ógrynni
match	maki
matter	mál, máli
may	Má, mætti, mega, megi, mundi
me	mér, mik
means	færi, tilföngum
meet	fund, hittast, mót, móts
meeting	móti
men	gumna, menn, mönnum, seggjum, virðar
merchant-voyages	kaupferðir
mercy	vægði
messengers	sendimenn
met	hittist
might	mátti
mind	hug
minds	huga
mine	minnar, mínum, mitt
missed	missa, misst
modestly	hæverskliga
more	fleira, meir, meira, meiri
morning	morgininn
most	flestum, mesta, mesti, mestu, mjök
most-beautiful	fríðust
most-prolific	prúðligsta
most-valiant	snjallari
mother	móðir, móður
mound	haug
mound-of-snow	hengiskafla
mourned	harmaði
mouth	munni
much	mikil, mikill, mikinn, mikit, mikla, miklar, miklu, miklum, mjök
Muli (place)	Múla
murder	morðráð
must	Mun
my	mína, minnar, minni, mínu, mínum, mitt
myself	mik

N, n

English	Old Norse
named	heita, heitir, hét, nefnd, nefndr
near	hjá, nær
nearly	náliga
neck	hálsinn
need	þurfti
needed	þarf, þurfa
neither	hvárki
never	aldri, aldrigi
new	nýju
news	tíðenda, tíðendi, tíðendin, tíðendum
next	næst
night	nætr
no	ekki, engan, engi, nú
noble	göfga, göfugr
noble-like	göfugligum
nobly	höfðingliga
none	eigi, engi
nor	né
not	eigi, Ekki, engi
now	Nú

O, o

English	Old Norse
obey	hlýða
obliged	skyldari

Word List (English to Old Norse)

English	Old Norse	English	Old Norse
obtained	aflaði	particularly	einkum
Oddi (name)	Odda, Oddi	parting	skilnaðr
Oddi's (name)	Odda	passed	liðit
of	á, af, at, er, í, of, ok, þar	passes	leið
		path	götuna, stíg
of-age	aldrs	peace	friðaði
of-all	öllum	people	drótt, mannval, menn, mönnum, þjóða
off	af		
offered	bauð	people-felled	mannfall
of-Goths	Gauta	people-felling	mannfallit
of-him	hans	person	mann, manni
of-marriage-grown	gjafvaxta	place	laut, stað, stóð
often	oft	placed	staddr, staðit
of-the-Goths	gauzkrar	places	staði
of-the-journey	fararinnar	planned	stofnat
of-them	þeira	poet	skáld
of-this	þessa	poetry	kvæðinn
of-you	yðr	poetry-making	kveðskaprinn
old	gamall	poet's-reward	skáldskaparlaunum
older	eldri	pointed-out	vísaði
on	á, í	possessions	föng
one	Annarr, Annat, einn, eins, einum, eitt, enn	power	föng, orku, vald
		praise	lofsorð, mærði
one-day	sinn	praised	lofuðu
only	eiga, eina, einn	precious	dýrar
or	eða, eðr	preparation	viðbúnaði
or-else	ella	preparations	búit
other	aðra, annars	prepare	búa
others	aðrir, öðru, önnur	prepared	búa, búins, búit, skipuð
otherwise	annars, ella, elligar		
our	vár, várr	presents	presentur
ours	unz	prestige	tígn
out	út, úti	prevail	ráða
out-from	út	princely	tígnar
out-of	ór	protection	nát
outrages	illvirki	provisions	liðskosti
over	of, ofan, yfir		
overboard	útbyrðis		
overcome	yfirkoma		

Q, q

English	Old Norse
over-going	ofangöngunni
owned	átt, eignaði
ownership	eigu

| queen | dróttningar |
| quickly | skjótast, skjótt, snarráðir |

P, p

Word List (English to Old Norse)

English	Old Norse
R, r	
rage	eiskranlig
raided	herjar
raiding	hernað, hernaði
raised	hafiðr
ran	hljóp
rather	heldr, helzt
reached	næðist
reaction	Bregðr
ready	búnir, greiða
realm	sýslu
recited	kveðit
redeem	kaupast
regarded	þykkja
remarkable	merkiligsti
remembered	minntist, mundi
repay	launa
report	títt
respectable	sómasamligri
responsibility	ábyrgð
retainers	hirð
returning	aftr
reward	launa
Reykjardal (place)	Reykjardal
rich	ríkar
riches	auði
right	drótt, dróttar
rings	hringa
rode	riðu
rough	snarpri
roughly	snarpri
ruled	réð
ruler	jöfra
ruling	Réð, stjórna
S, s	
said	játti, kvað, kvaðst, kváðu, sagði, sagðist, sagt, seggir, segir, segja, sögðu, talði
sail	siglu
sail-danger	seglhættu
sake	sakir
same	sama
sat	sat, sett, settr
saw	sá, sæi, sák, sjá
say	seggja, segja
saying	máli
search	leita
searching	leita
seaweed	þangi
see	líta, sjá
seek	sækja
seeking	leita
seem	þykkja
seemed	sýndist, þætti, þótti, Þóttist, þykkir
seems	sýnist, þykkir
seen	sá, sén, sét
sending-men	Sendimenn
sent	sendi, sendir
separate	skiljast
set	setr, sett, setti, settr
shall	skal
shared	deili
sharply	snarpir
she	hana, henni, hér, hon
sheathed-sword	Skeið
she-wolf's-head	ylgjarhöfuð
shield	skildi
shield-maiden	skjaldmær
shield-maidens	skjaldmeyja, skjaldmeyjar
shimmering	skjóma
ship	barð
ship-fleet	skipaflota, skipaflotann
ships	skip
ship-steering-man	skipstjórnarmaðr
shoe-thong	skóþvenginn, skóþvengr
short	skjóta
shortage	skorta, skorti
shorter	skemr, skjótara
should	mun, muni, skilði, skuluð, skyldi
show	lýsa
sickness	sótt, sóttin

Word List (English to Old Norse)

English	Old Norse
side	megin
sides	megin
sister	systir
sit	sitja
skills	list
slayings	vígaferði
sleep	svefni
slept	sofnaði, sofnar
small-stones	smágrjót
so	a, sá, sem, sjá, Slíku, Sú, svá, svát
so-as	at
soft-bed-prepared	umbúnaðr
sold	seldr
some	Sumir
someone	nökkurr
something	nökkur, nökkut
some-time	eitthvert, nökkut
somewhat	nökkur, nökkurs, nökkut
son	son, sonar, sonr
son-of-Helgi (name)	Helgason
soon	brátt, snemma
soonest	skjótast
sorcery	fjölkynngi
so-that	svát
sought	leit, leitaðist, sækja
sound	sundunum
speak	talar
spear	skaftl
spear-guardian	geirvaldr
spears	geiri, vigrum
speech	máli
spite	böls
spoke	kvað, kvaðst, mælt, mælti, mæltu
spoken	mælt
stain	Áta
standing	staddir, standa
star	stjörnu
Star-Oddi (name)	Stjörnu-Odda, Stjörnu-Oddi
stars	stjörnur
start	hefjast
statements	ráð
steered	stýrði
stem	stofni
stepped	sté
stewards	sýslumenn
stiff-footed	stirðr
stood	staddr, staðit, stóð, stóðu
storm	hríðmál
straight	drjúgt
straightaway	þegar
strain	hneig
strength	afli, magni
stricken-sun	hnigsólar
striking	hjuggu
striking-distance	höggfæri
strong	sterkr
struck	höggr
subduing	brýtr
subjects	þegnum
such	slíka, slíks, slíku, slíkum, svá
such-like	þvílíks
summoned	kvatt
supervision	umsjá
swooping	Svipun
sword	hjörs, sverði, sverðinu
swords	sverða

T, t

English	Old Norse
take	taka, takast
taken	taka, tekinn
takes	tekst
tall	hátt
teeth	tönnum
telling	sagði, sögu
temple	Hofs
Temple-Head (place)	Höfða, Hofshöfði
tens	tugum
test	reyna
than	en, í
thanked	þakkaði, þakkar
that	á, að, at, en, enn, er, hinn, hvat, sá, sem, þann, þar, þat, þeiri, þetta, til

Word List (English to Old Norse)

English	Old Norse	English	Old Norse
the	á, at, en, er, í, in, ina, inn, inni, ins, inum, it, Þat, þau, þess, þessi, þetta	*the-king's*	konungrinn, konungs, konungsins, siklings
		the-king's-men	konungsmönnum
the-assembly	þing	*the-king's-poet*	konungsskáld
the-battle	bardaga, bardaginn, orrostunni	*the-king's-ship*	konungsskipinu, konungsskipit
the-berserkers	berserkjanna, berserkjunum	*the-king's-sister*	konungssystir
		the-land	landi, landinu, lands, lönd
the-best	hezt	*the-lands*	lands
the-blow	höggit	*the-land's-people*	landsfólkit
the-bodies	hold	*them*	þeim, þeir, þeira
the-border	mörkinni	*the-matter*	máli
the-brothers	bræðir	*the-men*	ljónar
the-day	daginn	*the-most*	mest
the-dream	draum, drauminn, drauminum	*the-mound*	hauginn, hauginum
		themselves	sér, sik
the-earl	jarl, jarli, jarls	*then*	á, at, En, hina, Síðan, þá, þaðan, þann, Þar, Þat, því
the-earl's-daughter	jarlsdóttir		
the-evil-doers	illvirkjanna, illvirkjarnir		
the-feast	veizluna, veizlunni	*the-news*	tíðendi
the-fight	sameignar	*the-night*	nóttina
the-firth	firrðisk	*the-other*	annarr
the-forest	skóginn	*the-others*	inum
the-goddesses	Ásynju	*the-outlaw-men*	útilegumannanna
the-gods	véar	*the-people*	alþýðu, mönnum
the-government	landsstjórnin	*the-poem*	kvæði, kvæðinu, kvæðit
the-greatest	mestr		
the-guest	gestrinn	*the-poet*	skáld, skáldi, skáldinu, skálds
the-hand	handa		
the-helm	hjálmi	*the-queen*	dróttning, dróttningar, dróttningin
the-helmsman	hilmis		
the-highway	þjóðbrautinni	*there*	bar, þangat, Þar, þau, þeir, þeira, þeiri
the-hill	hólinn, hólinum		
the-house	húsinu	*therefore*	því
their	sín, sinna, sitt, þeira	*the-ring*	hringinn
theirs	sínum, þeira	*the-robbers*	stigamönnum
the-island	eyjarinnar	*the-robbing-men*	stigamannanna
the-journey	ferð, ferðinni	*the-saga*	sagan, sagði, söguna, sögunnar, sögunni
the-key	grafinn	*the-sake-of*	sakir
the-king	konung, konungi, konunginn, konunginum, konungr, konungrinn, konungs, konungsins, siklingi, siklingr	*the-same*	sæma, saman
		these	þenna, þessa, þessar, þessi, Þessir
		the-sea	Sjár
		the-ship	skipan, skipi
the-kingdom	ríki, ríkinu, ríkis, ríkit	*the-ships*	skipanna, skips
		the-ship's	skipa

Word List (English to Old Norse)

English	Old Norse	English	Old Norse
the-sound	sundin, sundunum	to-do	gera
the-stars	stjörnum	together	saman, samför
the-surf	lágarða	togetherness	samför
the-tables	borðum	to-have	láta
the-toast	erfinu	to-hear	áheyrsla
the-treasure	féit	to-her	henni
the-treasurer	gunndjarfr	to-him	hann, honum
the-truth	satt	to-know	vita
the-way	gata	told	getit, sagðak, sagði, sagt, talat, tölðu
the-weather	veðri		
the-wedding	brúðhlaup	told-of	getit
the-wicked	svikmenni	to-me	mér
the-woman	kvenna	to-meet	hitt
they	Þær, þar, Þat, Þau, þegar, þeim, þeir, þeira	too	of
		took	leiðir, næmdu, nam, takast, tekr, tók, tókust
they-are	eru		
they-were	Váru	toothed	tindótt
things	hluta, hluti, hlutum	to-other	öðrum
think	Hugsat, hygg	to-travel	fara
thinking	hugr	toughness	harðfengi
thirty	þrítug	to-you	þér, yðr
this	sú, þat, þenna, Þess, þessa, þessar, þessarar, þessari, þessi, þessu, þessum, þetta	traditions	sið
		travel	færi, far, fara, farandi, farar, ferðina, fóru
		travelled	fara, ferr, fór, fórst, fóru
this-king	konungrinn	travelling	farit, ferðina
thong	þvenginn	travel-weary	farmóðr
Thord (name)	Þórðr	treasure	fé, fyrða
though	þó, þótt, þóttist	treasured	dýrmörum
thought	hug, hugði, hugðu, mundi, þætti, þótt, þótti, þóttist, þóttust, þykki	trees	börva, við
		trollish	tröllsligt
		trolls	Trölls
		trust	treysta
three	þrjú	truthful	sannsögull
throne	stól	turned	snýr
through	ór	twelve	tólf
throw	skjóta	two	tvá, tveggja, tveir
thrown	varp		
tied	bindr		
time	tíma, tímar		
times	sinni		
t-look	sjást		
to	á, af, at, en, í, svá, þat, til, vit		
to-be	verða		

U, u

English	Old Norse
un-alert	ósnöfrmannliga
un-courteous	ólát
under	und, undan, undir

Word List (English to Old Norse)

English	Old Norse
unequal	ójafnað, ójafnari
unfolded	rekka
unheard-of	endemi
uninvited	óboðit
unlocked	luku
un-pleasant	ódælli
un-swinging	örvígr
until	unz
unusual	fáheyrðr
up	upp
upon	á
upright	rekkum
urged	fýstu
us	oss

V, v

English	Old Norse
valiant	böðfrækn
various	ýmissa
verse	vísur
verses	vísur
very	einkar
victory	sigr, sigri
victory-gift-gods	sigrgöfgaðir
viking	víking
viking-raids	víking
vikings	víkinga, víkingar
virtuous	dyggir
vision	fyrirburðr, víst
visions	fyrirburð
visit	vitja
voyage	ferðar

W, w

English	Old Norse
wafting	hváfta
wake	vakni
wall	vegg
wanted-to	vill
war-clothes	herklæðum
war-company	herliði
warfare	herför, vígroða
warrior	gramr
warriors	drengir, gramr, grams
was	enn, er, eru, sem, væri, var, varð, váru, vera
was-heard	spyrjast
was-named	hét
waves	bylgjur
way	leið, veg, venja
ways	vega
wealth	fé, fjár, fjárins
wealthy-treasures	auðæfum
weaponed	vápnaðir
weapon-nimble	vápnfimi
weapons	vápnum
weapons-exchange	vápnaskipti
weight	vægis
well	allvel, vel
went	færi, fór, för, fóru, gekk, gengr, gengu
were	er, væri, var, váru
we-sailed	Sigldum
what	en, er, hvat, hverra
when	er
where	er, hvar
which	en, er, sem
while	hríð, meðan
who	er, Hver, hverr
whole	heilum
wide	breiðan, víða
widely	víða
wield	valda
wife	eiginkonu, kona, konu
wife-of	kona
will	vil, vill
willed	vildi, vildu, vilja
willing	fúsastr
will-you	villtu
windswept	byrsóta
winters	vetra
wise	fróðr, vitr, vitrustum
wisest	vitrasta
wish	vil, vili, vilið, vill
wished	vildi, vildu
with	at, enda, með, of, ór, við, víða
within	innan
without	útan

Word List (English to Old Norse)

English	Old Norse
woke	vaknaði
woken	vaknat
wolf	heiðingja
wolf's	ylgjar
woman	kona, kvenna
woman's-customs	kvennasið
women	konur
won	gagn
wonder	undr, undrast
wonderful	ágætum
wonder-like	undarligr, undarligt
wood	skíð, víði
worded	orð, ort
words	mála, orð, orða
word-struggle	orðahjaldr
working-man	verkmaðr
worth	verðr, virðing
worthily	virðuliga
worthiness	virðing, virðingu
worthy	verða, virðing, virðuligr, virðuligri
would	munda, mundi, mundu, muni
would-be	væri
wounds	sárum
written	ritnar

Y, y

English	Old Norse
yet	Þó
you	þér, þik, þú, yðr
young	ung, unga, ungr
your	yðvarrar, yðvarri
yours	þín
yourself	sjálfum
youth	æsku

The Tale of Star-Oddi's Dream (*Old Icelandic*)

Old Icelandic	Literal	English
1	**1**	**1**
Þórður hét maður er bjó í Múla norður í Reykjardal.	Thord was-named a-man who lived at Muli in-the-north in Reykjardal.	There was a man named Thord who lived at Muli in the north, in Reykjardal.
Þar var á vist með honum sá maður er Oddi hét og var Helgason.	There was in hospitality with him so a-man who Oddi named and was Son-of-Helgi.	There was a man living with him named Oddi who was the son of Helgi.
Hann var kallaður Stjörnu-Oddi.	He was called Star-Oddi.	He was called Star-Oddi.
Hann var rímkænn maður svo að engi maður var hans maki honum samtíða á öllu Íslandi og að mörgu var hann annars vitur.	He was calendar-computation-wise a-man so that no man was his match him contemporary in all Iceland and that many was he otherwise wise.	He was skilled in the art of calendar computation, such that no man in all of Iceland was a match for him, and he was also wise in many other things.
Ekki var hann skáld né kvæðinn.	Not was he poet nor poetry.	He was not a poet, nor did he know much poetry.
Þess er og einkum getið um hans ráð að það höfðu menn fyrir satt að hann lygi aldrei ef hann vissi satt að segja og að öllu var hann ráðvandur kallaður og tryggðarmaður hinn mesti.	This was also particularly told about his statements that it had people before the-truth that he lied never if he knew the-truth to say and that all was he honest called and faithful-man the most.	It was also particularly said about him of his statements that people held them to be the truth, that he never lied if he knew the truth to tell, and that he was the most honest and faithful man.
Félítill var hann og ekki mikill verkmaður.	Fee-little was he and not much working-man.	He was poor and not an especially good worker.
Frá því er að segja að um þenna mann Odda gerðist undarlegur atburður.	From therefore is to say that about this man Oddi happened extraordinary events.	The story goes that extraordinary events happened to this man Oddi.
Hann fór heiman út til Flateyjar er Þórður húsbóndi hans sendi hann þessa ferð á vit fiska og er eigi annars getið en þeim fórst vel til eyjarinnar.	He travelled home out-from to Flatey when Thord housemaster his sent him this journey to to fishing and was not anything-else told-of but they travelled well to the-island.	He travelled out from his home to Flatey when his housemaster Thord sent him on a journey to go fishing, and nothing else is told except that the journey to the island went well.
Þar var hann í góðum beina.	There was he in good assistance.	He was well looked after there.

The Tale of Star-Oddi's Dream (Old Icelandic)

Old Icelandic	Literal	English
Ekki er frá því sagt hver þar bjó.	Not was from therefore said who there lived.	It was not said who lived there.
En frá því er að segja að um kveldið er menn fóru í rekkju var vel búið um Odda og hæglega.	Then from therefore was it said that about evening were people going to bed was well preparations about Oddi and comfortable.	Then from there it was said that about one evening people were going to bed, as preparations were made to make Oddi comfortable.
En við það er Oddi var farmóður og veittur hóglegur umbúnaður þá sofnar hann brátt og dreymdi hann þegar að hann þóttist staddur vera heima í Múla og svo þótti honum sem þar væri kominn maður til gistingar og þótti honum sem menn færu í rekkju um kveldið.	And with that was Oddi was travel-weary and given comfortably soft-bed-prepared then slept he soon and dreamed he straightaway that he though stood was home in Muli and so seemed to-him that there was come a-man to guest and thought he as people went to bed about evening.	And with Oddi being travel-weary, he was given a comfortable and soft bed that had been prepared for him, and he soon fell asleep and dreamed straightaway that he stood at home in Muli, and it seemed to him that a man had come as a guest, and that people were going to bed in the evening.
Þótti honum gesturinn vera beðinn skemmtanar en hann tók til og sagði sögu og hóf á þessa leið.	Seemed to-him the-guest was asking entertainment and he took to of the-saga telling and began in this way.	It seemed to him that the guest had asked for some entertainment, and he took to telling a saga, which began in this way.

2

Old Icelandic	Literal	English
Hróðbjartur hefir konungur heitið.	Hrodbjart had king dominion.	Hrodbart had the rule of a king.
Hann réð austur fyrir Gautlandi.	He ruled east for Götaland.	He ruled over east Götaland.
Hann var kvongaður maður.	He was married man.	He was a married man.
Hildigunnur hét kona hans.	Hildigunn named wife his.	His wife was named Hildigunn.
Þau áttu sér einn son barna er Geirviður er nefndur.	They had themselves only son child was Geirvid was named.	They had an only child whose was named Geirvid.
Hann var snemma vænn og vitmikill og að öllum hlutum mannaður um fram sína jafnaldra en barn var hann að aldri er sagan gerðist.	He was soon handsome and knowing-much and in all things brought-up about from his equal-age but child was he of age when the-saga begins.	He grew up to be handsome and wise in all things more than those his age, but he was a child when the saga begins.

The Tale of Star-Oddi's Dream (Old Icelandic)

Old Icelandic	Literal	English
Frá því er að segja að konungurinn Hróðbjartur hafði settan til landstjórnar yfir þriðjung ríkis síns jarl þann er Hjörvarður hét.	From therefore is to say that this-king Hrodbjart had appointed to governing over a-third-of kingdom his earl then was Hjorvard named.	From there is to say that this King Hrodbjart had appointed an earl to govern over a third of the kingdom who was named Hjorvard.
Hann var og kvongaður og hét kona hans Hjörgunnur.	He was also married and named wife his Hjorgunn.	He was also married and his wife was named Hjorgunn.
Þau áttu eina dóttur barna.	They had only daughter child.	They had a daughter who was an only child.
Sú hét Hlégunnur.	So named Hlegunn.	She was named Hlegunn.
Frá henni er svo sagt að hún var ólát í æsku sinni og var ávallt því ódælli sem hún var eldri.	From her is so said that she was un-courteous in youth hers and was always therefore un-pleasant as she was older.	It is said of her that she was discourteous in her youth and got more unpleasant as she got older.
Það var og sagt að hún vildi ekki kvenna sið fága í sínu athæfi.	It was also said that she willed not woman customs cultivate in her behaviour.	It was also said that she did not wish to cultivate womanly traditions in her behaviour.
Það var hennar venja jafnan að hún gekk í herklæðum og með vopnum og ef hana skildi á við menn þá veitti hún þeim annaðhvort áverka stóra eða líflát þegar henni líkaði eigi.	It was her way always that she went in war-clothes and with weapons and if she should then against people then gave her them either-way injury great or life-less as-soon-as she liked not.	It was always her way that she went about in armour with weapons, and if people went against her in any way she gave them either a great injury or death as soon as she did not like them.
En við þenna hennar ójafnað þá þótti Hjörvarði jarli föður hennar eigi mega við sæma hennar vandræði og sagði henni þá ljóslega að hann mundi eigi þann veg lengur láta fram fara og kvað henni eigi hlýða mundu nema um batnaði nokkurs háttar	Then with this her unequal then thought Hjorvard the-earl father hers not may with the-same her difficulty and told her then lightly that he may not then way longer let from go and said she not obey would except about bettering somewhat kind	Then with this overbearing behaviour, her father earl Hjorvard felt that he may not tolerate her disruptions any more, and told her plainly that it could not go on any longer, and that she should do somewhat better,
"eða ellegar far í brott sem skjótast úr minni hirð".	"or otherwise travel to away as soonest from my court".	or otherwise leave my court as soon as possible.

The Tale of Star-Oddi's Dream (Old Icelandic)

Old Icelandic	Literal	English
En þegar Hlégunnur jarlsdóttir verður þessa áheyrsla af föður sínum að hann vildi hana láta í burt fara af sinni hirð þá svarar hún því máli svo að hún kvað sig þar ekki dvelja og beiddi hún þá föður sinn að hann skyldi fá henni langskip þrjú alskipuð bæði að mönnum og herklæðum og búa að öllu sem best með góðum liðskosti svo að henni þætti vel skipuð.	Then as-soon-as Hlegunn the-earl's-daughter became of-this to-hear of father hers that he willed her leave to away travel from his court then answered she therefore saying so that she spoke herself there not dwell and asked she then father hers that he should give her longships three fully-prepared both in men and war-clothes and prepare that all as best with good provisions so that she seemed well prepared.	Then as soon as the earl's daughter Hlegunn came to hear of her father, that he wished her to travel away from his court, then she answered therefore declaring, that she did not wish to stay there and asked her father to give her three longships fully prepared with men and armour, and prepared with the best provisions so that she was well prepared.
Og ef svo væri gert sem hún beiddi hér um þetta mál þá taldi hún sér mundu vel líka þótt hún færi í braut við svo búið.	And if so would-be done as she asked she about that matter then said she herself would well like thought she travel to away with so prepared.	And if it would be done as she asked in this matter then she said she would like to travel away as she was prepared.
Hjörvarður jarl vildi gjarna þetta til vinna að hún kæmist á braut sem skjótast því að honum þótti, sem var, mikil vandræði af standa hennar ráði.	Hjorvard the-earl willed gladly this to grant that she comes to away as quickly therefore that he thought that was much difficulty of standing her conduct.	Earl Hjorvard was glad to grant this so that she would go away as soon as possible, for he thought there was great difficulty with her conduct if she stayed.
Síðan lét hann búa að öllu þrjú langskip sem best.	Then had he prepared to all three longships as best.	Then he had prepared all three longships as best as possible.
En þegar þetta lið var búið þá fer Hlégunnur jarlsdóttir úr landi með þessu liði og lagðist síðan í hernað og víking og aflaði sér svo fjár og frama.	Then as-soon-as the crew were prepared then travelled Hlegunn the-earl's-daughter out-of land with this crew and lay afterwards to raiding and viking and obtained herself such wealth and fame.	Then as soon as the crew were ready Hlegunn the earl's daughter travelled out of the land with this crew and went raiding and viking and obtained such wealth and fame for herself.
Svo er sagt að hún kom eigi í land meðan faðir hennar lifði.	So was said that she came not to land while father hers lived.	So it was said that she did not come back to the land while her father lived.

The Tale of Star-Oddi's Dream (Old Icelandic)

Old Icelandic	Literal	English
En í annan stað er þar til að taka sögunnar að þá er Geirviður son Hróðbjarts konungs var átta vetra gamall tók Hróðbjartur konungur sótt og verður það lítil frásaga því að sóttin leiðir svo til lands að konungurinn andast.	But in another place is there to of take the-saga that then was Geirvid son Hrodbjart's king was eight winters old took Hrodbjart king sickness and became that little from-to-say accordingly that sickness took so to the-lands that the-king died.	But to take the saga to another place, then King Hrodbjart's son Geirvid was eight winters old, Hrodbjart took ill, and there was little to say of it, but a sickness took to the land and the king died.
Það þótti öllum hans ástvinum og virktamönnum hinn mesti skaði, sem var, að missa slíks höfðingja og þar út í frá öllu landsfólkinu.	That thought all of-him beloved and chosen-man the most harm, as was, that missed such chieftains and there out to from all lands-folk.	Everyone thought this a great harm as he was beloved by his chosen companions, chieftains, and people of the land.
Síðan var fengið að virðulegri veislu og þar til boðið öllum hinum ríkustum mönnum og hinum bestum höfðingjum er í voru landinu.	Afterwards was got then worthy feast and there to invited all the kingdom's people and the best chieftains that in were the-land.	Afterwards a worthy feast was prepared, and all of the kingdom's people and the best chieftains in the land were invited.
Þar með var og til boðið hverjum manni þeim er veisluna vildi sækja, bæði innan lands og utan svo að engi skyldi þar óboðið koma.	Then with was also to invited each person they of feast willed seek, both within lands and without so that none should there uninvited come.	With that, everyone who wished to attend was also invited, both within the land and without, so that no one should come uninvited.
En síðan þessi veisla var saman sett með því fjölmenni er þangað sótti þá var þar erfi drukkið eftir Hróðbjart konung með miklum veg og sóma svo sem byrjaði hans tign og sómasamlegri virðingu.	Then after the feast were together set with because followers were there attending then was there a-toast drunk after Hrodbjart the-king with much way and honour so as began his prestige and respectable worthiness.	Then after the feast was held with the many followers who attended there, a toast was drunk for King Hrodbjart, in such a way that honoured his prestige and respectable worthiness.
En er erfinu var lokið þá var konungurinn heygður að fornum sið eftir því sem þá var tíska til við göfga menn.	Then as the-toast was ended then was the-king buried in ancient traditions after according-to as then was fashion to with noble men.	Then when the toast had ended, the king was buried according to ancient traditions that were then fashionable with noble men.

The Tale of Star-Oddi's Dream (Old Icelandic)

Old Icelandic	*Literal*	*English*
3	**3**	**3**
Nú er svo að segja að eftir þessi miklu tíðindi er þar í landi höfðu gerst þá sýndist það öllum hinum vitrustum mönnum og hinum bestum vinum konungsins að taka annan mann til konungs og landstjórnar í stað þvílíks höfðingja sem þá var við misst.	Now is so to say that after this much news was there in the-land had done then seemed that all the-others wise people and the best friends the-king's to take another person to king and governing the place such-like chieftains as then were with lost.	Now the saga goes that after this there was much news in the land that all the wise people and the king's best friends had to take another person as king and for the chieftains to cover the place as such a leader had been lost.
En svo var mikil ástúð öllum landsmönnum á Hróðbjarti konungi meðan hann lifði að menn vildu ekki annað en velja Geirvið son hans til konungs og láta eigi konungdóminn ganga úr hans ætt.	But so was great affection of-all lands-people to Hrodbjart the-king while he lived that people willed not another to choose Geirvid son his to king and allowed not kingdom going out-of his lineage.	But so great was the affection of all the people of the land to King Hrodbjart while he lived that no one wanted to choose other than Geirvid his son as king and not to let the kingdom pass out of his lineage.
Þótt Geirviður væri ungur að aldri eða hann þætti þá enn lítt til landráða fallinn í þann tíma vildi þó allt landsfólkið til þessa hætta með umsjá drottningar móður hans með því að hún var hin vitrasta kona og vel að sér í alla staði.	Thought Geirvid was young in age and he thought then that little to land-ruling disposed in that time willed though all the-land's-people to this conclude with supervision queen mother his with accordingly that she was the wisest woman and well to herself in all places.	Though Geirvid was young in age and seemed little disposed to ruling the land at that time, all the people of the land wished it, with supervision of his mother the queen accordingly, as she was the wisest woman and capable in all ways.
En er svo fór fram um hríð að svo ungur maður skyldi höfðingi vera og stjórna mörgu fólki sem Geirviður var þá gerðist brátt landstjórnin lítil, sem líklegt var.	But when so went from about awhile that so young man should chieftain be and ruling many folk as Geirvid was then became soon the-government little, as likely was.	But when this had been so for a while, with such a young man as Geirvid being a ruler and governing many people, then the government became weak, as was likely.
Það gerðist og að hirðin fáttkaðist fyrir því að margir voru þeir af hans hirðmönnum að aðra iðn lögðu fyrir sig.	It became also that courtiers few because therefore that many were they of his court-men that other crafts laid for themselves.	It also came about that he courtiers were fewer because many of his court men found themselves other jobs.
Sumir lögðust í víking, aðrir réðust í kaupferðir til ýmissa landa.	Some laid to viking-raids, others appointed to merchant-voyages to various lands.	Some went on viking raids, others were appointed on merchant voyages to various lands.

The Tale of Star-Oddi's Dream (Old Icelandic)

Old Icelandic	Literal	English
Nú með því að á þessu þótti mikið mein sem nú var frá sagt þá gerðust þó mörg önnur óhægindi í ríki þessa hins unga konungs.	Now with therefore that of this thought much harm as how was from said then made though many others inconvenience in the-kingdom this the young king.	Now with this being thought of as much harm, as before said, then there were other inconveniences in the kingdom of this young kind.
Þess er við getið í sögunni að illvirkjar tveir lögðust út á skóg þann er Jöruskógur heitir.	This was with told-of in the-saga that evil-doers two camped out in forest then was Battle-forest named.	It was told of in this saga that two evil doers camped out in the forest which was then named Battle Forest.
Það var í ríki þessa hins unga manns.	It was in kingdom this the young man's.	This was in the young man's kingdom.
Þessir víkingar drápu menn til fjár sér og voru nálega berserkir.	These vikings killed people for wealth as also were nearly berserkers.	These vikings killed men for money and were virtually berserkers.
Annar þeirra hét Garpur en annar Gnýr.	One of-them named Garp and the-other Gny.	One of them was named Garp, and the other Gny.
Svo er sagt að mönnum hlýddi aldrei fám að fara saman.	So is said that people followed never few to travel together.	So it was said that people never travelled in small numbers together.
Jafnan voru menn vanir að fara á skóginn með fjölmenni að leita illvirkjanna og ráða þá af en þeir urðu aldregi hittir þó að þeirra væri leita farið með fjölmenni.	Always were people friends that travelled to the-forest with followers-many to search for-the-evil-doers and prevail then of which they became never found though that they were searching travelling with followers-many.	People were always travelling with friends to the forest with followers to search for these evil doers and defeat them, but they were never found, even though many people were searching for them.
Slíku fer fram til þess er Geirviður konungur er tólf vetra.	So it-went from to this that Geirvid the-king was twelve winters.	So it went on until King Geirvid was twelve winters old.
Og þá er hann var svo aldurs kominn þá var hann svo mikill maður vexti og sterkur að afli sem þeir menn margir sem fullkomnir voru að aldri og atgervi nálega eftir því sem þeir best voru á sig komnir fyrir allra hluta sakir.	And then when he was so of-age come then was he so much a-man grown and strong in strength as they men many as fully-come were to age and deeds closely after accordingly which they best were in himself come before all things sake.	And then when he had come of age, he was a great man in height and strength, as much as many men who had come of age, and almost like those who were at their peak in all things.

The Tale of Star-Oddi's Dream (Old Icelandic)

Old Icelandic	Literal	English
Það var eitthvert sinn þá er Geirviður konungur sat yfir borðum með allri hirð sinni, þá tók hann til orða og mælti svo:	Then was some-time one-day then that Geirvid the-king sat over the-tables with all retainers his, then took he to words and spoke so:	Then one day King Geirvid sat at the table with his retainers, and took to words and said:
"Nú er svo sem yður er kunnigt öllum mínum mönnum að eg hefi ungur verið hér til að aldri og svo hefi eg haft litla orku og því hefir af mér staðið lítil stjórn í ríkinu.	"Now is so as you that known all my men that I have young been forces to that age and so have I had little power and therefore have of me stood little control in the-kingdom.	Now it is well known to you, all my people, that I have been young and have had little power, and therefore I have had little control over the kingdom.
Hefi eg það og oft heyrt sem von er að.	Have I that and often heard as expected was it.	And I have often heard, as was expected,
Má það og eigi mjög undrast þó að hér til hafi af mér lítil stjórn staðið fyrir sakir æsku minnar.	May it also not much wonder though that forces to have of me little control placed before the-sake-of youth mine.	It may also not be much to wonder that I have had little force of control for the sake of my youth.
En þó er eg nú svo aldurs kominn að mér er nú mál að reyna mig og vita að nokkuð vilji mitt ráð þroskast og meir hefjast en áður er þar sem eg er nú orðinn maður tólf vetra gamall.	However though am I now so of-age come that to-me is now matter to test myself and know that something wish mine decide develop and more start then after that there was I am now become a-man twelve winters old.	However, now that I have come of age, there is now the matter to test myself and I wish to know something whether it is decided that my rule will develop and become more after than it was at the start, now that I am a man of twelve winters old.
Eru og margir ekki betur mannaðir á mínum aldri.	Are and many not better mannered at my age.	There are many my age who are not better mannered than me.
Nú vil eg og því lýsa fyrir öllum yður, mínum þegnum og virktavinum, að eg ætla mér að fara til móts við berserkina, þá Garp og Gný, er liggja á Jöruskógi og gera þar mörg illvirki.	Now will I also therefore show for all of-you, my subjects and friends, that I intend me to travel to meet with berserkers, then Garp and Gny, who camped in Battle-forest and do there many outrages.	Now therefore I wish to show all of you, my subjects and friends, that I intend to travel to meet with the berserkers, Garp and Gny, who camp in Battle Forest and do many outrages there.
Ætla eg og til þess að koma eigi aftur svo að þeir séu á lífi og skal eg þá yfirkoma eða þeir mig ella".	Intend I also to this that come not back so so-as they are of alive and shall I then overcome or they me or-else".	I also do not intend to come back so long as they are alive, and either I shall over come them, or they me".

The Tale of Star-Oddi's Dream (Old Icelandic)

Old Icelandic	Literal	English
En er Geirviður konungur hafði þetta mælt þá svarar fyrst máli hans drottningin móðir hans og þar með allir hans bestu menn og mæltu nálega allir sem eins manns munni og báðu konung fara fjölmennan á fund stigamannanna og með miklum viðbúnaði ef hann vildi fara.	And when Geirvid the-king had this spoke then answered first speech his the-queen mother his and there with all his best people and spoke almost all as one man's mouth and asked the-king travel followers-many to find the-robbing-men and with much preparation if he wished to-travel.	And when King Geirvid had spoken, the first to answer his speech was his mother the queen, along with his best people, and all spoke almost with one voice and asked that the king travel with many followers to find the robbing men and with much preparation if he wished to travel.
Geirviður konungur svarar:	Geirvid the-king answered:	King Geirvid answered:
"Hugsað hefi eg þetta mál áður nokkuð fyrir mér en eg kvæði upp og sýnist mér á þá leið sem í þessari ferð megi mér þá engi frami kaupast þótt eg fái náð berserkjunum enda leita eg þeirra með miklu liði alvopnuðu.	"Think have I this matter before some-time for me that I announced up and seems to-me that then passes so in this journey may for-me then not courage redeem though I get protection the-berserkers with seeking I them with much company all-weaponed.	I have been thinking about this matter for some time before I announced it and it seems to me that if it so passes on my journey, I may not redeem courage if I have the protection from the berserkers while seeking them with a great company all armed.
En það er þá nokkur svívirðing ef þeir fást þá eigi og komi eg við það aftur og verður þá ósnöfurmannlega minnar handar ef svo tekst.	But it is then somewhat disgraceful if them get then not and come I with it returning and became then un-alert my hand if so takes.	But then it is a disgrace if they are not caught, and I will come to return, and then it will have been feeble for my hand if it it ends like that.
Nú hefi eg hina leið ætlað ferðina að fara með annan mann á þeirra fund og mun þá skipta gæfa með oss hver þá skal verða vor skilnaður.	Now have I then company intend travelling that travel with another person that they find and should then exchange good-fortune with us each then shall become our parting.	Now I intend to travel with another person to find them, and it should then exchange good fortune between us and we shall se how we part.
Má þá og verða ef vill að nokkur svo fremd fylgi ferðinni.	May then also be if will that something so honour follows the-journey.	May it then also become, if willing, that some honour follows this journey.
Skal nú og á það ráð hætta hversu sem til vill takast.	Shall now also to that decide conclude how-so as to will take.	That shall now decide and conclude how it may turn out.

The Tale of Star-Oddi's Dream (Old Icelandic)

Old Icelandic	Literal	English
Er nú og fyrir því upp borið þetta mál fyrir yður að eg vil nú vita hver fúsastur er til þessarar ferðar með mér og er nú það ráð að nokkur vakni við, sá er til vill ráðast, og svari sá nú mínu máli enda skuluð þér það vita hér með að nú er þetta mál fullgert fyrir mína hönd að eg mun þó fara þessa ferð þótt eg fari einn saman og verði engi til að fylgja mér".	Is now also before because up brought this matter before you that I wish no to-know who willing that to this journey with me and is now that decision to someone wake against, so that to wish arrange, and answer so now my speech and should you it know here with that now is this matter full-done before my hand that I should though travel this journey though I travel one the-same and be none to that follow me".	Now, therefore, this matter has been brought before you that I now want to know who is most willing to go on this journey with me, and it is now the plan that someone will wake up, whoever may decide, and he will now answer my question, and you shall do so. Know herewith that now this matter is settled on my behalf that I will still go on this journey even though I go alone and there will be no one to follow me".
En við þessi ummæli konungs þá er það sagt að drottning sjálf fyrst að upphafi latti á alla vega þessar ferðar og sagði, sem var, allóráðlega stofnað þar sem við heljarmenn var að eiga er illvirkjarnir voru, svo mikið sem þar var í ábyrgð er konungurinn var sjálfur því að öllum þótti vís von að hann mundi látast fyrir þeim og fá minna hlut í þeirra skiptum ef svo yrði sem líklegt mundi þykja fyrir sakir æsku konungs þeirra en harðfengi berserkjanna.	And with these about-words the-king's then was it said that the-queen herself first to became discouraged to all ways this journey and said, that was, all-un-forethought planned there as with accursed-men was that only were criminals were, so much as there was in responsibility was the-king's was himself therefore to all thought aware expecting that he would die before them and get less lot of there exchanged if so became as likely would regarded for sake youth the-king's they which toughness the-berserkers.	And with these words from the king, then it was said that the queen herself was the first to discourage this expedition in every respect, and she said it had been planned with little forethought, with these accursed men who were criminals, as much as there was a responsibility for the king himself, all expected that he would get the worst of it and die because of them, if it became as was likely, for the sake of the king's youth and the toughness of the berserkers.
Allir vinir konungs löttu ákaflega fararinnar og þótti konungur út seldur ef hann færi við annan mann.	All friends the-king's dissuaded extremely of-the-journey and thought the-king out sold if he journeyed with another man.	All the king's friends were extremely discouraging of the journey and thought that the king would be done for if he went with only one other man.
Konungur svarar að ekki mundi tjóa að letja hann.	The-king answered that not would avail to discourage him.	The king answered that it would be to no avail to try and discourage him.
Og er allir skildu að konungur mundi eigi letjast láta þá verður til og svarar máli konungs sá er Dagfinnur hét.	And when all knew that the-king would not discouraged allow then became to also answer the-matter the-king's so that Dagfinn named.	And when all understood that the king would not be discouraged, then cane an answer to the king's case, who was named Dagfinn.

77

The Tale of Star-Oddi's Dream (Old Icelandic)

Old Icelandic	Literal	English
Hann var hirðmaður konungs og konungsskáld.	He was court-man the-king's and the-king's-poet.	He was the king's court man and the king's poet.
"Herra", segir hann, "engan mann veit eg þér meiri sæmd eiga að launa í alla staði en mig.	"Lord", said he, "no person know I to-you more honour have to reward in all places than me.	"Lord," said he, "I know of no man more honorable to you in all things than me.
Er eg og því skyldari að skiljast aldrei við þig er þú ert í meira háska staddur ef þér viljið þiggja mitt föruneyti og fylgd og er eg til þessar farar albúinn þegar þér viljið".	Am I also therefore obliged to separate never with you that you are the more danger placed if you wish accept my companionship and follow and that I to this travel all-prepared as-soon-as you wish".	I am therefore more obliged to never part with you when you are in more danger if you want to accept my entourage and escort, and I am ready for this journey whenever you want".

4

En þegar þessi maður, Dagfinnur, var nefndur í sögunni þá er frá því að segja er mjög er undarlegt að þá brá því við í drauminum Odda að hann Oddi sjálfur þóttist vera þessi maður, Dagfinnur, en gesturinn sá er söguna sagði er nú úr sögunni og drauminum en þá þóttist hann sjálfur sjá og vita allt það er héðan af er í drauminum.	Then as-soon-as this man, Dagfinn, was named in the-saga then was from accordingly to say that much was wonder-like that then drew therefore with in the-dream Oddi's that he Oddi himself thought was this man, Dagfinn, but the-guest so was the-saga telling was now out-of the-saga and the-dream and then thought he himself so and knew all that was from-here of for in the-dream.	But when this man, Dagfinn, was mentioned in the story, it is very strange to say that in Oddi's dream it happened that Oddi himself thought he was this man, Dagfinn, but the guest who told the story is now out of the story and the dream, but then he thought he saw and knew all that is henceforth in the dream.
En nú síðan er drauminn svo að segja sem honum þótti sjálfum fyrir sig bera, Odda, þá þóttist hann vera Dagfinnur og ráðast í ferðina með konunginum Geirviði.	Then now after in the-dream so to say as he thought himself before himself borne, Oddi, then thought he was Dagfinn and arranging to travel with the-king Geirvid.	But now since the dream is, so to speak, that Oddi then he thought he was Dagfinn and embarked on the journey with King Geirvid.
En er þeir voru albúnir þá riðu þeir tveir saman með vopnum sínum til þess er þeir komu á Jöruskóg þangað sem illvirkjanna var von en þar var svo viður vaxið að gata var breið um skóginn.	Then when they were all-prepared then rode they two together with weapons theirs to this that they came to Battle-forest from-there as the-evil-doers were expecting then they were so trees grown that the-way was broad about the-forest.	Then when they were ready the two rode together with their weapons until they came to Battle Forest, where the evil doers were waiting, then the trees were so grown that there was a wide path through the forest.

The Tale of Star-Oddi's Dream (Old Icelandic)

Old Icelandic	Literal	English
Og er þeir komu mjög langt í skóginn þá er þess getið að þar varð fyrir þeim hóll einn mjög hár.	And when they came much long in the-forest then is this told-of that there was before them hill one much high.	And when they came very far into the forest, it is told that there was a very high hill before them.
Hann var brattur öllum megin.	It was broad all sides.	It was steep on all sides.
Síðan gengu þeir upp á hólinn og vildu þaðan sjást um og vita hverra tíðinda þeir mættu vísir verða.	Afterwards went they up by the-hill and wished then t-look about and know what news they may know to-be.	Then they went up the hill and from there wanted to look around and know what tidings they might become.
Mart smágrjót var á hóli þessum.	Many small-stones were on hill this.	Many small stones were on this hill.
Þaðan sáu þeir víða.	From-there saw they widely.	From there they saw widely.
Þeir geta að líta hvar ganga tveir menn.	They could to look where going two men.	They could see where the two men were walking.
Þeir voru miklir vexti og gengu þegar þangað að hólinum sem þeir konungur stóðu.	They were great grown and went they from-there to the-hill as they the-king stood.	They were tall and they immediately walked to the hill where the king stood.
Þessir menn voru báðir vel vopnaðir.	These men were both well weaponed.	These men were both well armed.
En þegar þeir konungur og Dagfinnur sáu þessa menn þá þóttust þeir vita að þar voru þeir komnir Garpur og Gnýr.	Then as-soon-as they the-king and Dagfinn saw these men then thought they knew that there were they coming Garp and Gny.	But when the king and Dagfinn saw these men, they thought they knew that Garp and Gny had come there.
Þá mælti Dagfinnur:	Then spoke Dagfinn:	Then Dagfinn said,
"Herra, eg vil yður kunnigt gera að eg er eigi mjög vanur vopnaskipti og kann eg lítt að treysta hug mínum né vopnfimi.	"Lord, I wish to-you know be that I am not much accustomed weapons-exchange and can I a-little to trust mind mine nor weapon-nimble.	Lord, I want to let you know that I am not very accustomed to exchanging arms, and I can scarcely trust my mind or my agility.
Nú vil eg að þér kjósið um tvo kosti, hvort þér viljið heldur að eg ráðist í mót berserkjunum með þér eða viltu að eg sjái til yðvarrar sameignar af hólinum og kunni eg frá að segja öðrum mönnum".	Now wish I that you choose about two benefits, either you wish rather that I determine to meet the-berserkers with you or will-you that I see that your fight of the-hill and know I from to say to-other people".	Now I want you to choose two options, whether you want me to attack the berserkers with you or you want me to see to your fight from the hill and I can tell other people what happened".

The Tale of Star-Oddi's Dream (Old Icelandic)

Old Icelandic	Literal	English
Konungur svarar:	The-king answered:	The king answered:
"Ef þér lér nokkuð tveggja huga um þetta mál þá þykir mér einsætt að þú sért hér á hólinum og sjáir héðan til sameignar vorrar og komir eigi nær við vor vopnaskipti".	"If you lean somewhat two minds about this matter then seems to-me evident that you are here on the-hill and look from-here to the-fight aware and come not near with our weapons-exchange".	If you lean somewhat in two minds about this matter, I think it is decided that you are here on the hill and see from here to the fight and do not come any closer to our exchange of arms.
Dagfinnur tekur það ráð sem konungur mælti og dvaldist eftir á hólinum og kemur hvergi nær og þykir honum það allráðlegt en konungurinn sjálfur ræðst ofan af hólinum í móti stigamönnunum.	Dagfinn took this advice as the-king spoke and dwelled afterwards on the-hill and came each near and seemed to-him that advisable what the-king himself decided over of the-hill in meeting the-robbers.	Dagfinn took the advice which the king had said and stayed on the hill, and came nowhere near, and he thought it wise, but the king himself attacked from the top of the hill against the robbers.
Þar kann eigi glögglega frá að segja hversu högg fóru með þeim og mun eg þar gera skjóta frásögu því að það er þar frá lyktum að segja að svo skipti hamingjan með þeim, því að konungi varð lagið líf og lykka, að hann bar af báðum illvirkjunum og létust þeir af stórum sárum er konungur hafði þeim veitt.	There known not clearly from to say how-so blows went between them and should I there do short from-saying because that it was there from completion to say that so exchanged graciousness with them, because that the-king was granted life and luck, that he bore of both evil-doers and had they of great wounds that the-king had them given.	It is not clear from there how the blows went with them, and I will make a quick account of it, for it is from there to say that their happiness that was so important to them was exchanged, for the king was given life and happiness, that he bore from both evil doers. and they died of the great wounds which the king had inflicted on them.
Og eftir það er illvirkjarnir voru fallnir þá gengu þeir konungur og Dagfinnur fram á götuna lengra og komu þar að farandi er stígur lítill lá af þjóðbrautinni í skóginn.	And afterwards that when the-evil-doers were fallen then went they the-king and Dagfinn from to path longer and came there to travel where climbed little lying of the-highway in the-forest.	And after the evildoers had fallen, the king and Dagfinn went further out into the path, and came to a place where a small path lay from the highway into the forest.
Þeir höfðu litla stund gengið þann hinn litla stíg áður brátt gerðist rjóður mjög mikið í mörkinni og stóð þar eitt hús.	They had little awhile gone then the little path before soon became clearing much greatly in the-border and stood there one house.	They had walked the small path for a short time before soon there was a lot of clearing in the border and a house stood there.
Það hús var hátt og rammgert og rammlega læst og grafinn lykill í dyragætti.	The house was tall and firmly-built and firmly locked and the-key buried in doorway.	That house was tall and firmly built, and firmly locked with a key buried in the doorway.

The Tale of Star-Oddi's Dream (Old Icelandic)

Old Icelandic	Literal	English
Þeir luku upp húsinu og gengu þar inn.	They unlocked up the-house and went they in.	They opened the house and went inside.
Það hús var vel innan búið og var nálega fullt af allskyns auðæfum.	The house was well inside prepared and was nearly full of all-kinds-of wealthy-treasures.	That house was well furnished and was almost full of all kinds of riches.
Þar voru þeir um nóttina og skorti þar hvorki góðan drykk né dýran mat en um morguninn fóru þeir heimleiðis og huldu áður hræ útilegumannanna.	They were there about the-night and shortage of neither good drink nor fine food then about morning travelled they homeward and covering after corpses the-outlaw-men.	They were there during the night and there was no shortage of good drinks or expensive food, but in the morning they went home and hid the carcasses of the outlaw men before.
En er konungurinn kom heim til ríkis síns þá varð hann frægur mjög víða um lönd af sínu þrekvirki og ágætum sigri og urðu allir vinir konungsins og frændur honum fegnir er hann kom heim með göfuglegum sigri og þóttust menn hann nálega úr helju heimt hafa, sem var.	Then when the-king came home to kingdom his then was he famous much with about the-land of his brave-deeds and wonderful victory and became all friends the-king's and kinsmen his celebrated that he came home with noble-like victory and thought people he nearly out-of Hel drawn had, as was.	But when the king came home to his kingdom, he became famous in many lands for his endurance and excellent victory, and all the king's friends and relatives rejoiced when he came home with a noble victory, and it was thought that people had almost recovered him from hell, which they were.

5

Nú eftir þenna atburð allan saman lét konungur þings kveðja og kemur þar mikið fjölmenni saman.	Now after these events all together had the-king an-assembly called and came there great many-followers together.	Now after all these events, the king called an assembly and a great many people gathered there.
En er saman var sett þetta hið fjölmenna þing þá sagði konungur þar þessi miklu tíðindi og þótti öllum þetta hin mesta frægð, sem var, er Geirviður konungur hafði einn sigur borið af slíkum kempum.	Then when together were sat that the many-men the-assembly then said the-king there this great news and thought all this the most fame, which was, that Geirvid the-king had one victory carried of such champion.	And when this large assembly was convened, the king there told this great news, and it was considered by all to be the greatest fame, which was that King Geirvid had won one such a battle.

The Tale of Star-Oddi's Dream (Old Icelandic)

Old Icelandic	Literal	English
Síðan bað Geirviður að menn skyldu vitja til þess húss er illvirkjarnir höfðu í borið það mikla fé og skyldi þar hver taka sitt fé það er misst hafði.	Afterwards invited Geirvid that people should visit to the house where the-evil-doers had in bore that much wealth and should there each take his wealth that was missed had.	Then Geirvid asked that men should visit the house in which the evildoers had brought much money, and that each should take his money which he had lost.
En allir gáfu konungi upp sitt fé það sem hver átti og sögðu það best komið að hann hefði og kváðu hann fullu kostað hafa.	But all have the-king up their wealth that which each had and said that best came to him have and said he fully earned had.	But they all gave to the king what they had, and said that it was best for him to have it, and said that he had earned it in full.
Síðan lét konungur sækja féið og kastaði á sinni eigu.	Afterwards had the-king sought the-treasure and cast to his ownership.	Then the king fetched the money and cast it into his possession.
Eftir það lét konungur taka til húsgerðar og gerðu menn konungi haug þann er hann skyldi sitja á.	After that had the-king taken to house-builder and made people the-king a-mound then that he should sit on.	After that the king had a house built, and the people made a mound for the king to sit on.
Þá var konungur settur á stól þann er stóð á hauginum og hófu menn hann svo einkum til tignar og gáfu honum þá enn af nýju dýrar presentur og dýrkuðu hann sem þeir höfðu framast föng á.	Then was the-king sat on throne then as place on the-mound and had people him so especially to princely and gave him then but of new precious presents and adored him as they had foremost possessions of.	Then the king was placed on the throne that stood on the mound, and the people began to honor him, and gave him again expensive gifts, and worshiped him whom they had bestowed.
Þess er við getið þar sem Dagfinnur skáld er, honum kom í hug að engi mundi skyldari til konunginn að sæma með kvæði en svo sem hann var.	This is with told-of that as Dagfinn the-poet was, he came to mind that none would obliged to the-king to honour with a-poem than such as he was.	This is told of Dagfinn the poet, that it occurred to him that no one would be more obliged to the king to honour with a poem than he was.
Síðan gengur Dagfinnur á hauginn upp til konungsins og féll á kné fyrir hann og laut honum og kvaddi hann virðulega og sagði honum að hann hefði kvæði ort um konunginn og bað að hann mundi hlýða.	Afterwards went Dagfinn on the-mound up to the-king and fell to knee before him and place his and greeted him worthily and said to-him that he had a-poem worded about the-king and asked that he would listen.	Then Dagfinn went to the mound up to the king and fell on his knees before him and bowed to him and greeted him respectfully and told him that he had written a poem about the king and asked him to listen.
Konungur játti því blíðlega.	King said accordingly joyfully.	The king agreed joyfully.
Síðan tók Dagfinnur til og flutti kvæðið og var það flokkur.	Then took Dagfinn to and brought the-poem and was it flokk.	Then Dagfinn took over and performed the poem, and it was a flokk.

The Tale of Star-Oddi's Dream (Old Icelandic)

Old Icelandic	Literal	English
Og er lokið var kvæðinu þá þakkar konungur vel og allir þeir er við voru staddir og sögðu vel ort og svo sem sæmdi tign og virðing konungs þeirra.	And when ended was the-poem then thanked the-king well and all there was with were standing and said well worded and so as honour prestige and worthy king they.	And when the poem was finished, the king thanked well and all those who were present and said it was well written and so they honored the prestige and worthiness of their king.
Og sem konungur heyrði að allir létu vel yfir og lofuðu mjög kvæðið þá vildi hann sér láta og verða stórmannlega og launa höfðinglega og vill gefa skáldinu gullhring mikinn er hann hafði á arminum.	And as the-king heard that all had all over and praised much the-poem then willed he himself to-have and worthy great-man-like and reward nobly and wanted-to give the-poet a-gold-ring great that he had on arm.	And when the king heard that everyone had praised the poem very much, he wanted to be generous and reward the poet with a large gold ring that he had on his arm.
En Dagfinnur vildi eigi hringinn þiggja og sagði svo að honum var mikil öfúsa á því að hafa sóma og virðing af konunginum en fé kvaðst hann eigi þurfa að þiggja af honum og kallaði sig ekki skorta meðan hann héldi honum heilum	But Dagfinn wished not the-ring accept and said so that he was great gratitude that therefore to have honour and worth of the-king that treasure said he not needed to accept of him and claimed himself not shortage while he held him whole	But Dagfinn did not wish to accept the ring and said that he was very grateful to have the honour and respect of the king, but he said he did not need to accept it from him because he had no shortage of anything as long as he kept him safe,
"en þeir eru margir aðrir er þar sjá til fjárins sem þér eruð".	"but there are many others that there look to wealth as to-you are".	but there are any others who look for wealth while looking to you.
Konungi líkar þetta vel.	The-king liked this well.	This pleased the king.

6

Þessu næst er að segja frá þeim tíðindum að Hjörgunnur kona Hjörvarðar jarls tók sótt hættlega og þarf þar eigi að gera mikinn orðahjaldur að þessi sótt leiðir Hjörgunni til bana.	This next was to say from they news that Hjorgunn wife-of Hjorvard the-earl took sickness dangerously and needed there not to do much word-struggle that this sickness took Hjorgunn to death.	The next thing to tell of news was that Hjorgunn, the wife of Earl Hjorvard, took a dangerous sickness and there is no need to struggle with words to say that this sickness took Hjorgunn to her death.
Síðan var hún erfð og út borin og gert eftir hana sem tíska var til í fornum sið eftir ríkar konur.	Afterwards was she honoured and out brought and made after her as fashion was to in ancient traditions after rich women.	Afterwards she was honoured and brought out and so it was done for her in the fashion of ancient traditions of wealthy women.

The Tale of Star-Oddi's Dream (Old Icelandic)

Old Icelandic	Literal	English
Jarli þótti mikill skaði eftir drottning sína, sem von var, og harmaði hana mjög og svo margir aðrir út í frá.	The-earl thought much harm after the-queen himself, as expected was, and mourned her much and so many others out in from.	The earl thought great harm to his queen, which was expected, and mourned her greatly, along with so many others from then on.
Eigi höfðu liðið langir tímar áður vinir hans fýstu að hann skyldi fá sér annarrar konu.	Not had passed long time before friends his urged that he should get himself another wife.	It had not been long before his friends wanted him to have another wife.
Hann spurði hvar þeir sæju honum kvonfang það er honum væri virðing í að fá.	He asked where they saw him a-match that was to-him being worthy in to get.	He asked where they saw for him a wife that he would be honored to receive.
Þeir töldu ráðlegt að hann bæði til handa sér Hildigunnar drottningar og sögðu honum mikið uppheldi að þeim ráðahag ef hann næðist.	They told advice that he ask for the-hand he Hildigunn the-queen and said to-him much advancement that they marriage-proposal if he reached.	They thought it advisable for him to ask for the hand of Queen Hildigunn, and said that there would be much advancement for him if such a marriage could be achieved.
Og er þetta var oft tjáð fyrir jarli þá sýndist á þá leið því að hann var vitur maður.	And was that was often expressed before the-earl then seemed to then laid therefore that he was wise man.	And when this was often told to the earl, he saw things the same way, because he was a wise man.
Síðan hefir hann upp orð sín og biður Hildigunnar drottningar sér til eiginkonu.	Afterwards had he up worded his and invited Hildigunn the-queen herself to wife.	Then he raised his words and asked Queen Hildigunn to marry him.
Hún var þá enn ekki meir en fertug kona að aldri og þótti kosturinn vera hinn merkilegasti fyrir allra hluta sakir.	She was then was not more than forty woman in age and thought distinguished was the remarkable before all things sake.	She was still no more than forty women at the time and was considered the most remarkable option for all intents and purposes.
Og hvort sem um þetta var talað lengur eða skemur þá var það að ráði gert að drottning var gift Hjörvarði jarli með ráði konungs sonar hennar.	And how as about this was told longer or shorter then was it that decision made that the-queen was married Hjorvard the-earl with consent the-king son hers.	And whether this was talked about longer or shorter, it was decided that the queen should marry Earl Hjorvard, with the consent of her son the king.
Síðan var fengið að virðulegri veislu og drukkið brúðhlaup Hjörvarðar jarls og Hildigunnar drottningar með miklum veg og margskonar sóma.	Afterwards was got a worthy feast and drank the-wedding Hjorvard the-earl and Hildigunn the-queen with much way and many-kinds-of honour.	Then a worthy feast was held, and the wedding of Earl Hjörvarður and Queen Hildigunn was drunk with great prestige and many honours.

The Tale of Star-Oddi's Dream (Old Icelandic)

Old Icelandic	Literal	English
Og er veislunni var lokið þá fer hver heim til sinna heimkynna.	And when the-feast was concluded then travelled each home to their households.	And when the feast was over, everyone went home to their households.
Brátt takast þar miklar ástir í millum þeirra og eru samfarar þeirra sæmilegar og eigi langar áður en þau áttu dóttur.	Soon took there much love in between them and was interaction theirs honourable and not long after then they had a-daughter.	Soon there was much love between them and their interaction was honourable, and it was not long after that they had a daughter.
Hún var nefnd Hlaðreið.	She was named Hladreid.	She was named Hladreid.
Svo er sagt að samför þeirra jarls og drottningar var eigi löng þaðan í frá er þau höfðu Hlaðreiði getið áður þau tíðindi gerðust að jarl tekur sótt og leiðir hún svo til lands að hann andast af þeirri sótt.	So was said that togetherness theirs the-earl and the-queen was not long from-there to from when they had Hladreid told before the news made that earl took sickness and led it so to the-land that he died of that sickness.	So it was said that the togetherness of the earl and the queen did not last long after they had Hladreid, before the news came that the earl had taken ill, and so it led through the land, and he died of that sickness.
Það þótti vera skaði mikill því að hann var virðulegur höfðingi.	It thought was harm much because that he was worthy chieftain.	It was thought a great harm because he was a worthy chieftain.
Eftir þessi tíðindi setti Geirviður konungur sína menn yfir ríkið það er jarl hafði átt og eignaði sér.	After this the-news set Geirvid the-king his men over the-kingdom that the earl had owned and owned himself.	After these tidings King Geirvid put his men over the kingdom which the earl had owned and appropriated.
Þessi tíðindi spyrjast víða, sem von var, fráfall þvílíks höfðingja.	This news was-heard widely, as expected was, death such-like a-chieftain.	These tidings were widely learned of, as was to be expected, from the demise of such a ruler.
Þar kemur að þessi tíðindi koma fyrir Hlégunni dóttur Hjörvarðar jarls, að faðir hennar er andaður, þar sem hún er í hernaði og brýtur undir sig víkinga.	There came to this news came before Hlegunn daughter Hjorvard the-earl, that father hers had died, there as she was about raiding and subduing under herself vikings.	There came these tidings to Hlegunn, the daughter of Earl Hjorvard, that her father was dead, as she was at war and subduing vikings.
Bregður henni svo við tíðindin að hún snýr öllu sínu liði til Gautlands og herjar þar.	Reaction hers so with news that she turned all her company to Götaland and raided there.	She reacted to the news by turning all her army towards Götaland and raided there.
Og svo kemur því máli að hún lagði undir sig allt það ríki er átt hafði faðir hennar.	And so came therefore the-matter that she had under herself all that kingdom which owned had father hers.	And then it came to pass that she subdued all the kingdom which her father had possessed.

The Tale of Star-Oddi's Dream (Old Icelandic)

Old Icelandic	Literal	English
Síðan sendir hún menn á fund Geirviðar konungs og bað svo segja honum sín orð að hann skyldi annaðhvort gera að unna henni hálfs ríkis og landráða við sjálfan sig eða ella skyldi hann búa sig og sína menn og koma til móts við hana með sinn her í sund þau er heita Síldasund og berjast við hana þar og hefði það þeirra sigur og gagn er meiri gæfu stýrði.	Afterwards sent she men to find Geirvid the-king and asked to say to-him her words that he should another-either do to grant her half the-kingdom and land-ruling with herself his or either should he prepare himself and his men and come to meet with her with her army in a-sound there was named Herring-sound and battle with her there and had that there victory and won was more luck guided.	Afterwards she sent men to find Geirvid and asked them to tell him her words, that he should either grant her half the kingdom and authority to rule or prepare himself and his men to come to meet with her army in a sound that was named Herringsound and battle with her there, and that victory would be won by whoever had the most luck.

7

Nú er þar til að taka að sendimenn fóru þeir er Hlégunnur sendi.	Now is there to to take the messengers travelled they that Hlegunn sent.	Now we take to the messengers that Hlegunn had sent.
Það voru skjaldmeyjar.	They were shield-maidens.	They were shield-maidens.
Þær fóru á konungs fund og báru upp sín erindi fyrir konunginn.	They went to the-king meet and brought up their errand before the-king.	They went to meet the king and presented their message to the king.
Og er hann heyrði kostaboð Hlégunnar þá svarar hann skjótt á þessa leið:	And when he heard choice-bid Hlegunn's then answered he quickly to this laid:	And when he heard Hlegunn's offer, he answered quickly in this way:
"Því skjótara skal kjósa sem kostir eru ójafnari og vil eg miklu heldur berjast við hana en láta ríki mitt fyrir ágangi hennar".	"Because shorter shall choices which choose they-are unequal and will I much rather fight with her than lose kingdom mine before aggression hers".	I shall sooner choose the more unequal option, and I would much rather fight against it than leave my kingdom to its invasion.
Sendimenn fóru aftur á fund Hlégunnar og segja henni til svo búins og líkaði henni þeirra för forkunnlega vel.	Sending-men travelled returning to meet Hlegunn and said to-her to so prepared and liked her their journey exceedingly well.	The messengers went back to meet Hlegunn and told her what had happened and she was pleased with their journey very much.

The Tale of Star-Oddi's Dream (Old Icelandic)

Old Icelandic	Literal	English
Nú er það að segja að Geirviður konungur safnar herliði um allt sitt ríki og skal hver maður fara í þessa herför er skildi má valda eða skafti skjóta.	Now is it to say that Geirvid the-king gathered war-company about all his kingdom and shall each man travel to this warfare who shield may wield or spear throw.	Now it is said that King Geirvid gathered armies all over his kingdom, and every man should go on this campaign whether he can carry a shield or throw a spear.
Þess er við að geta að höfði sá gekk einum megin hjá sundunum er Hofshöfði heitir og skyldi þar hittast lið konungsins allt við höfðann.	This is with to get that headland that went one side near the-sound was Temple-Head named and should there meet company the-king's all with headland.	It is now worth getting that the headland that went on one side near the sound was named Temple-Head and the king and his forces were all to meet at the headland.
En er Geirviður konungur var albúinn þá leiddi hann alþýðu til skips.	And when Geirvid the-king was all-ready then led he the-people to the-ships.	But when King Geirvid was ready, he led the people to the ships.
Þar var í ferð með konungi Dagfinnur skáld.	There was on the-journey with the-king Dagfinn the-poet.	The poet Dagfinn was on the journey there with the king.
En í ofangöngunni til skipanna þá varð sá atburður er geta verður, þó að lítils vægis þyki vera, að losnaði skóþvengur Dagfinns skálds.	But in over-going to the-ships then was seen happening which could worth, though that little weight thought being, that loosened shoe-thong Dagfinn's the-poet.	But in the passage to the ships, the event that can be mentioned, even though it is considered to be of little importance, was that the poet Dagfinn's shoelace came loose.
Og síðan bindur hann þvenginn og þá vaknaði hann og var þá Oddi, sem von var, en eigi Dagfinnur.	And after tied he thong and then woke he and was then Oddi, as expected was, and not Dagfinn.	And then he tied the shoelace, and then he awoke, and it was Odd, as was expected, but not Dagfinn.
Eftir þenna fyrirburð gekk Oddi út og hugði að stjörnum sem hann átti venju til jafnan er hann sá út um nætur þá er sjá mátti stjörnur.	After these visions went Oddi out and thought that the-stars which he had habitually to always that he saw out about night then was saw might stars.	After these visions Oddi went out and thought about the stars which he had always seen many of at night.
Þá minntist hann á drauminn og mundi allan nema kvæðið það er hann þóttist ort hafa í drauminum nema þessar vísur sem hér eru ritnar:	Then remembered he the dream and thought everything except the-poem that which he thought worded had in the-dream except this verse which here they-are written:	Then he remembered the dream and remembered everything except the poem he thought he had written in the dream except these verses written here:
Voru austr *á Jöruskógi* *barmar tveir*	They-were east in Battle-forest brothers two	There were in the east at Battle Forest two brothers

The Tale of Star-Oddi's Dream (Old Icelandic)

Old Icelandic	Literal	English
böls um fylltir	spite about filled	filled with spite
og til fjár	and to wealth	and for wealth
fyrðar næmdu	treasure took	they took treasure
við morðráð	with murder	with murder
mörgu sinni.	many times.	many times.
En sá gramr	But that warrior	But that anger
er gera bræðir	that made the-brothers	that the brothers made
hefir tírgjarn	had fame-ambition	had fame ambition
tindótt hjarta	toothed heart	with toothed heart
og böðfrækn	and valiant	and valiant
báða felldi	both felled	felled both
Garp og Gný	Garp and Gny	Garp and Gny
Geirviðr konungr.	Geirvid the-king.	King Geirvid.
Réð jafngjarn	Ruling equally	Ruling equally
auði að skipta	riches to divide	dividing the riches
Roðbjartssonr,	Son-of-Hrodbjart,	Hrodbjart's son,
rekka mærði	unfolded praise	unfolded praise
af því fé	of for wealth	of that wealth
fyrða kindir	among-people kin	among people and kinsmen
er svikmenni	that the-wicked	that the wicked
safnað höfðu.	gathered had.	had collected.
Lét gunndjarfr	Had the-treasurer	the treasurer had
gefna hringa	given rings	given rings
seggja ætt	say descendants	say descendants
siklingr Gauta	the-king Of-Goths	of the king of the Goths
svo að hirðmenn	so that court-men	so that the court men
höfðu allir	had all	had all
haukastóls	hawk-seat	a hawk's seat
hengiskafla.	mound-of-snow.	on a mound of snow.
Mun Dagfinnr	Must Dagfinn	Dagfinn must
dýrra málma	dear words	with dear words
við lofsorð	with praise	and with praise
lúka kvæði.	conclude the-poem.	conclude the poem.
Njóti vel	Appreciate well	Enjoy well
vegs og landa	glory and land	glory and land
gramr göfugr	warrior noble	noble warrior
gauskrar þjóðar.	of-the-Goths king.	king of the Goths.

The Tale of Star-Oddi's Dream (Old Icelandic)

Old Icelandic	*Literal*	*English*
8	**8**	**8**
En sem Oddi hafði úti verið slíka stund sem honum vel líkaði fór hann inn í rekkju sína og sofnaði þegar og dreymdi hann það sem hið fyrra sinn og hann hafði vaknað frá.	And as Oddi had out been such awhile as he well liked fared he in to bed his and slept immediately and dreamed he that which the first his and he had woken from.	But as Oddi had been outside for a moment which he liked well, he went into his bed and fell asleep at once, and dreamed it as the first time he had woken up from.
Þóttist hann þá hafa bundið skóþvenginn og vera Dagfinnur og skynda til skipanna.	Seemed to-him then had bound shoe-thong and was Dagfinn and hurrying to the-ships.	He then thought he had tied the shoelace and was Dagfinn and hurried to the ships.
Svo þótti honum í drauminum sem hann skyldi vera skipstjórnarmaður.	So seemed to-him in the-dream as he should be ship-steering-man.	In his dream, he thought he was a captain.
Og þegar þeir voru búnir til ferðar fóru þeir með skipaflotann til þess er þeir komu við höfðann og hittist þar allt lið konungs og lögðu síðan fram í sundin Síldasund.	And as-soon-as they were ready to voyage travel they with ship-fleet to this that they came with headland and met there all company the-king's and laid then from to the-sound Herring-sound.	And when they were ready to go, they took the fleet until they came to the head, and there met all the king's army, and then put into the channel Herring-sound.
Þá er og sagt að þar var komin Hlégunnur skjaldmær og lá þar fyrir í sundunum með skipaflota sinn og hafði ógrynni liðs og albúin til orustu.	Then is also said that there was coming Hlegunn shield-maiden and lying there before the sound with ship-fleet hers and had mass company and all-prepared to battle.	It is also said that Hlegunn, a shield-bearer, had arrived there and lay there in the channels with her fleet of ships, and had an innumerable army ready for battle.
Síðan lögðu hvorir í mót öðrum og laust saman með þeim snarpri sókn og var þar hinn harðasti bardagi og réðst brátt mikið mannfall í hvortveggja liði en þó hafði eigi lengi staðið bardaginn áður en mannfallið hneig í lið konungs og hruðust hans skip mjög.	Afterwards laid each to meet each-other and loosed together with they roughly attacked and was there the hardest battle and had soon much people-felled in each-way company but though had none longer stood the-battle before the people-felling strain to company the-king's and cleared his ships much.	Then they put up a fight against each other, and a sharp attack broke out with them, and there was the hardest battle, and soon many casualties were inflicted on both sides, but the battle had not lasted long before the casualty fell to the king's army, and his ships were greatly wrecked.

The Tale of Star-Oddi's Dream (Old Icelandic)

Old Icelandic	Literal	English
Þess er og getið að Hlégunnur varð ekki sén í orustunni um daginn og hugðu menn þó drjúgt að af konungsmönnum og þótti það undarlegt.	It is also told-of that Hlegunn was not seen in-the-battle about the-day and thought men though straight to of the-king's-men and thought that wonder-like.	It is also mentioned that Hlegunn was not seen in the battle that day, and yet many of the king's men thought of it, and thought it strange.
En er slíku hafði fram farið langa hríð um daginn þá leitaðist Dagfinnur um með sinni list og sá hann þá Hlégunni og var þá komin á konungsskipið og var þá orðin skipan mikil á hennar hag.	And when such had from gone long while about the-day then sought Dagfinn about with his skills and saw he then Hlegunn and was then come to the-king's-ship and was then become the-ship great about her circumstance.	But when such a thing had taken place for a long time that day, Dagfinn sought with his art, and he then saw Hlegunn, and had then come to the king's ship, and by then there had been a great order in her favour.
Honum sýndist á henni ylgjarhöfuð geysimikið og tröllslegt og biti með því höfuðin af konungsmönnum.	To-him seemed that her she-wolf's-head exceedingly-great and trollish and bit with against heads of the-king's-men.	It seemed to him that her head was a wolf's head, huge and trollish, and that it bit the heads of the king's men.
En er Dagfinnur sá þessi undur þá steig hann af því skipi er hann stýrði.	Then when Dagfinn saw this wonder then leapt he off then the-ship that he steered.	But when Dagfinn saw this miracle, he got off the ship he was steering.
Það lá fjarri konungsskipinu.	It lay far-away the-king's-ship.	It was far from the king's ship.
Síðan hljóp hann hvert af öðru uns hann kom á konungsskipið.	Afterwards ran he each of others until he came to the-king's-ship.	Then he ran one by one until he came to the king's ship.
En þegar hann kom á fund konungs þá sagði Dagfinnur hvað títt var og hvað stór endemi voru við.	Then as-soon-as he came to find the-king then said Dagfinn what report was and that great unheard-of was against.	But when he came to meet the king, then Dagfinn said what was to report and what a great unheard of thing they were up against.
Síðan vísaði Dagfinnur konungi til hvar Hlégunnur var, að hann mætti sjá hana, en konungur fékk hana eigi séð sakir fjölkynngi hennar en hitt sá hann að menn hans féllu tugum saman.	Afterwards pointed-out Dagfinn the-king to where Hlegunn was, that he may see her, but the-king got her not seen for-the-sake-of sorcery hers but found saw he that men his fell tens together.	Then Dagfinn referred to the king where Hlegunn was, that he might see her, but the king could not see her because of her witchcraft, but he saw that his men fell together by the dozens.
Þá bað Dagfinnur konunginn sjá undir hönd sér hina vinstri og svo gerði hann.	Then asked Dagfinn the-king look under hand his the left and so did he.	Then King Dagfinn asked the king to see under his left hand, and so he did.

The Tale of Star-Oddi's Dream (Old Icelandic)

Old Icelandic	Literal	English
En er konungur fór svo með þá sá hann Hlégunni.	And when the-king did so with then saw he Hlegunn.	But when the king went with him, he saw Hlegunn.
Síðan gengu þeir báðir saman aftan til siglu.	Afterwards went they both together aft to sail.	Afterwards went they both together aft to sail.
Þá hljóp konungurinn fram með brugðnu sverði og þegar hann kemur í höggfæri við Hlégunni þá höggur hann til hennar með sverðinu og kemur höggið á hálsinn og hjó hann af henni höfuðið og féll það útbyrðis.	Then ran the-king forwards with drawn sword and as-soon-as he came to striking-distance with Hlegunn then struck he to her with sword and came the-blow to neck and hewed he off her head and fell it overboard.	Then the king ran forward with a drawn sword, and when he came under attack with Hlegunn, he struck her with the sword, and the blow came on her neck, and he cut off her head, and it fell overboard.
En er hún var fallin þá bauð konungurinn kost þeim mönnum er fylgt höfðu Hlégunni hvort þeir vildu heldur halda bardaga upp við hann eða ganga honum til handa.	And when she was fallen then offered the-king choice they the-people who followed had Hlegunn each they willed rather hold battle up with him or go him to hand.	But when she had fallen, the king offered the men who had followed Hlegunn whether they would rather fight him or go to his hand.
En þeir kjöru skjótt að ganga á konungs vald.	Then they chose quickly to go to the-king's power.	But they soon chose to enter into the king's power.
Og síðan er Geirviður konungur lagði á braut úr þeim bardaga þá lagði hann undir sig allt landið og setur þar yfir sýslumenn og friðaði svo allt ríkið.	And afterwards when Geirvid the-king had to away from them the-battle then had he under his all land and set there over stewards and peace so all the-kingdom.	And since King Geirviður set out from that battle, he conquered the whole country and placed it over the magistrates, and then pacified the whole kingdom.
Síðan hélt konungur heim og var ger í mót honum dýrðleg veisla.	Afterwards held the-king home and was made to meet him glorious feast.	Then the king returned home, and a glorious feast was held for him.
Eftir það var kvatt þings og var það þing allfjölmennt.	After it was summoned assembly and was the assembly all-many-people.	After that an assembly was convened and that assembly was very crowded.
Var konungurinn Geirviður settur þá enn á stól af nýju og hafiður upp á hinn sama haug sem fyrr og nú til konungs tekinn og ríkisstjórnar yfir allt Gautland.	Was the-king Geirvid set then was on throne of new and raised up in the same mound as before and now to the-king taken and governor over all Götaland.	King Geirviður was then again put on a chair again and raised on the same mound as before and now taken to the king and the government over all of Götaland.

The Tale of Star-Oddi's Dream (Old Icelandic)

Old Icelandic	Literal	English
Gekk þá annar höfðingi að öðrum upp á hauginn og gerði til konungsins veg og sóma hver eftir slíku sem framast hafði föng og færi á.	Went then one chieftain to another up to the-mound and made to the-king way and honour each after such as foremost had power and means of.	Then another chieftain went up to the hill, and made a way for the king, and honored each one according to all that he had.
Dagfinni skáldi kom það í hug að engi átti konunginum meiri virðing að launa í alla staði en hann.	Dagfinn the-poet came to the thought that none had the-king more worthiness to repay in all places than him.	The poet Dagfinn thought that no one had more respect for the king in all respects than he.
Gekk hann síðan upp á hauginn og kvaddi konunginn vel og hæversklega.	Went he then up on the-mound and greeted the-king well and modestly.	He then went up to the mound and greeted the king kindly and modestly.
Konungur tók glaðlega kveðju hans.	King took gladly greeting his.	The king gladly accepted his greeting.
Dagfinnur sagði konunginum deili á því að hann hafði þá enn ort kvæði um hann af nýju og bað að hann skyldi hlýða og kvaðst þá vilja færa kvæðið.	Dagfinn told the-king shared that accordingly that he had then one worded a-poem about him of new and asked that he should listen and spoke then willed bring the-poem.	Dagfinn told the king that he had written a poem about him again, and asked him to listen, and said he would bring the poem.
Konungurinn svarar að hann kvaðst gjarna hlýða vilja.	The-king answered that he said gladly listen willed.	The king replied that he will gladly listen.
Tók þá Dagfinnur og flutti kvæðið og var það þrítug drápa er hann þóttist ort hafa.	Took then Dagfinn and brought the-poem and was it thirty drapa which he thought worded had.	Then Dagfinn took and recited the poem, and it was thirty stanza drapa which he thought he had written.
En er kvæðinu var lokið þá þakkaði konungur það allvel og dró digran gullhring af hendi sér og gaf Dagfinni að skáldskaparlaunum en Dagfinnur vildi eigi þiggja hringinn og sagðist allt ærið hafa meðan hann héldi konunginum heilum.	And when the-poem was concluded then thanked the-king it well and drew a-thick gold-ring of hand his and gave Dagfinn the poet's-reward but Dagfinn willed not accept the-ring and said all abundance had as-long-as he held the-king whole.	But when the poem was finished, the king thanked him very well and took a huge gold ring from his hand and gave Dagfinn a poet's reward, but Dagfinn did not want to accept the ring and said he had abundance as long as he kept the king whole.

The Tale of Star-Oddi's Dream (Old Icelandic)

Old Icelandic	Literal	English
En Geirviður konungur lét það þá í ljós við Dagfinn að hann skyldi hans sóma meira gera í alla staði heldur en hvers manns annars í sínu ríki og bauð honum það að hann mundi afla honum kvonfangs og sagði svo að hann mundi þá konu fá honum til handa er hann vildi helst kjósa, nálega þess er kostur var í því landi.	But Geirvid the-king had it then to light with Dagfinn that he should him honour more do than all places rather than each man other in his kingdom and offered him that to him would gain him a-match and said so that he would then a-wife get him to hand that he willed rather choose, nearly this as choice was in then the-land.	But King Geirvid then made it clear to Dagfinn that he should do him more honour in all respects than any other man in his kingdom, and offered him that he would give him a wife, and said that he would get a woman for him, which he preferred to choose, close by in the land whom Dagfinn most wanted to marry.
Dagfinnur tók þessu máli vel, sem von var, er konungurinn vildi svo mikinn gera hans sóma og svarar:	Dagfinn took this matter well, as expected was, as the-king willed so much to-do him honour and answered:	Dagfinn took this matter well, as was to be hoped, since the king wished so much to do him honour, and answered:
"Ef þetta skal allt efna af yðvarri hendi við mig sem nú er um mælt þá er ekki því að leyna að er sá kosturinn að gjarna mundi eg mér unna og þú átt og mest undir sjálfum þér".	"If this shall all be-carried-out of your hand with me as now is about spoken then is not because that concealing that is so choice that gladly would I to-me love and you have and the-most under yourself to-you".	If all this is to be done by your hand with me, as is now said, then it is no secret that the choice is that I would gladly treat myself and you have and most of all under yourself.
Konungur mælti:	King spoke:	The king said,
"Hver er sú kona er þú talar til?"	"Who is this woman that you speak to?"	Who is the woman you are talking to?
Dagfinnur svarar:	Dagfinn answered:	Dagfinn answered:
"Það er Hlaðreið systir þín.	"It is Hladreid sister yours.	It is Hladreid, your sister.
Hún er svo kvenna að mér er mestur hugur á að fá ella hygg eg að fyrir muni farast um kvonföngin".	She is so the-woman that to-me is the-greatest thinking that to marry otherwise think I that for should go about a-match".	She's so the woman that I'm most interested in marrying, otherwise I think about the match going".
Konungur sagði að það skyldi og eigi undan draga við Dagfinn er honum þótti sinn sómi vaxa við.	The-king said that it should and not under drawn with Dagfinn that he thought his honour grow with.	The king said that nothing should be denied to Dagfinn which he thought would increase his honour.

The Tale of Star-Oddi's Dream (Old Icelandic)

Old Icelandic	Literal	English
Hlaðreið konungssystir var þá gjafvaxta og þó ung mjög að aldri en kvenna var hún fegurst og fríðust og best að sér ger um alla hluti.	Hladreid the-king's-sister was then of-marriage-grown and though young much in age but woman was she fairest and most-beautiful and the-best that herself made about all things.	Hlaðreið, the king's sister, was then gifted and yet very young, but of women she was the most fair and beautiful and the best at everything.
En hvort sem þetta mál var talað lengur eða skemur þá ræðst það af að Hlaðreið var föstnuð Dagfinni skáldi.	And how as this matter was told longer or shorter then decided it of that Hladreid was betrothed-to Dagfinn the-poet.	But whether this matter was discussed longer or shorter, it was determined that Hladreid was engaged to the poet Dagfinn.
Síðan var þar fengið að boði og var þar ger hin veglegasta veisla í alla staði með hinum bestum tilföngum því að ekki vantaði til það er hafa þurfti.	Afterwards was there got to announced and was there done the greatest feast in all places with the best means because that not lacking to this was had need.	Then it was announced and there was the most successful feast in all respects with the best resources because there was no shortage of what was needed.
Þar var og allt hið besta mannval það er í var landinu.	There were also all the best people that were in were the-land.	There was also all the best selection of people in the country.
Var nú drukkið brúðhlaup þeirra með hinni mestu sæmd og prýði.	Was now drunk the-wedding they with the most honour and finery.	Their wedding was now drunk with the greatest honour and splendor.
En er veisluna þraut þá fór hver til sinna heimkynna er þangað hafði sótt.	And when the-feast finished then travelled each to their households that from-there had attended.	But when the feast ended, everyone who had gone there went to their own home.
En með þeim Dagfinni og Hlaðreiði tókust brátt miklar ástir og var þeirra samför einkar góð.	And between them Dagfinn and Hladreid took soon much love and were they together very good.	And between Dagfinn and Hladreidi, they soon fell in love and their relationship was very good.
En er svo kurteislega var komið ráðahag Dagfinns sem nú er frá sagt þá var lokið drauminum og vaknaði hann þá, er Oddi var raunar.	But when so courtly was come marriage Dagfinn's as now was from said then was ended the-dream and awoke he then, that Oddi was actually.	But when in such a courtly fashion had Dagfinn's marriage taken place, as related, the dream ended, and he awoke that was actually Oddi.

The Tale of Star-Oddi's Dream (Old Icelandic)

Old Icelandic	Literal	English
9	**9**	**9**
Síðan hugði Oddi að um draum sinn og mundi gersamlega drauminn allan, bæði hinn fyrra og svo hinn síðara, og minntist síðan á drápuna þá er hann þóttist síðar kveðið hafa og mundi hann eigi fleira í kvæðinu heldur en þessar ellefu vísur sem nú eru hér ritnar og þetta er upphaf að:	Afterwards thought Oddi that about dream his and remembered completely the-dream all, both the first and so the latter, and remembered afterwards the drapa then that he thought afterwards recited had and would he not more of the-poem rather than these eleven verses as now they-are here written and this is beginning of:	Then Odd thought of his dream and remembered the whole dream, both the first and then the second, and then remembered the drapa when he was thought to have recited later and he remembered no more in the poem than these eleven verses now written here and this is the beginning of:
Geirviðr of nam greiða gang svo að skreið úr þangi	Geirvid of took ready going so that glided through seaweed	Geirvid took ready going as gliding through seaweed
og byrsóta beitti barð út um lágarða. Og seglhættu sóttu snarpir meðr úr veðri,	and windswept biting ship out about the-surf. And sail-danger attended sharply between with the-weather,	and windswept biting a ship out and about in the surf. and danger attended the sails sharp with the weather,
blés við hún, und höfða,	blew with her, under Temple-Head,	blew against her under Temple Head,
harðan vegg of seggjum.	hard wall with men.	a hardened wall of men.
Skeið náði þá skríða	Sheathed-sword caught then action	The sheathed sword then caught ation
skjót um bylgjur ljótar. Fóru dyggir drengir á dýrmörum hlýra. Þar sá eg frægra fyrða för prúðlegsta görva. Þó er gotneskra gumna Geirviðr konungr þeira.	launched about waves hideous. Travelled virtuous warriors in treasured bows. There saw I famous fighters went most-prolific clearly. Yet of Gothic men Geirvid the-king theirs.	launched about hideous waves. Virtuous warriors travelled in treasured bows. There I saw famous fighters going most prolific and clearly. Yet of the Gothic men Geirvid is their king.
Sigldum Hofs fyrir höfða herðendr, skipaferðum, Göndul, grams, með landi,	We-sailed Temple before headland hardy, ship's-course, Göndul, warriors, with land,	We sailed to Temple Head before the Headland hardy, the ship's course, Gondul, the warriors, with the land,
gott ráð var það dróttar, uns í Síldasundi sigrgöfgaðir vigrum hjuggu horskir seggir hjörs andskota börva.	good advice was that right, ours in Herring-sound victory-gift-gods spears striking brave said sword enemies trees.	good advice that was right, until in Herring-sound victorious god gifted spears striking bravely said the enemy sword trees.

The Tale of Star-Oddi's Dream (Old Icelandic)

Old Icelandic	Literal	English
Og skjaldmeyja skjóma skerðendr svo gerðu að varfærir véar í vág fyrir lágu. Gátu ljónar líta leiðangrs flota breiðan. Hilmis fór und hjálmi, hirð, sú er vörn of firrðist.	And shield-maidens shimmering diminished so doing with caution the-gods in inlet before laying-to. Could the-men see expedition fleet wide. Helmsman went under the-helm, court-men, so were defended over the-firth.	And shield-maidens shimmering did so diminish with the caution of the gods in the inlet before laying-to. The men could see the expedition fleet wide. The helmsman went under the helm, The court men, so were defended over the firth.
Brátt vöknuðu virðar að vígboði þjóðar þá er Hlégunnar hestar hafrastar mjög þustu og snarráðir sóttu siklings vinir þingað. Þó er gotneskra gumna Geirviðr konungr þeira.	Soon awoke men that battle-bidding great-river then were Hlegunn's horses eagerly most flailing and quickly attended the-king's friends assembled. Yet of Gothic men Geirvid king theirs.	Soon awoke men to the battle-bidding people then were Hlegunn's horses eagerly most flailing and quickly attended the king's friends assembled. And yet of all the Gothic men, Geirvid was their king.
Og hnigsólar Högna hríð æxti þá síðan blóðísunga beiðir, bragna konr, af magni, en vígroða víða varp af rómu snarpri. Sjár varð dökkr af dreyra drótt þá er hríðmál sótti.	And stricken-sun Hogni's awhile increased then after blood-helmeted demanded, heroes descended, of strength, then warfare wide thrown of battle rough. The-sea became dark of gore people then were storm encountered.	And Hogni's stricken sun increased awhile, then afterwards the blood-helmeted demanded, heroes descended, of strength, then warfare wide thrown of battle rough. The sea became dark with gore people then were storm encountered.
Svipan gerðist þar sverða, saman kómu þar rómu, Göndul varð fyrir grundu, grams drótt því að vel sótti. Geirviðr of vó geiri, geirvaldr, í Hlökk þeiri. Blóðár sá ég í blóði. Blóð stökk um skör þjóða.	Swooping came there swords, together came there a-roar, Göndul became before ground, warriors right because that well attended. Geirvid too guarded spears, spear-guardian, in Looking-forward there. Bloodied saw I in blood. Blood leapt about across people.	Swooping came there swords, together came there a-roar, Göndul fell to the ground, warriors right because that well attended. Geirvid too guarded spears, spear-guardian in looking-forward there. Bloodied, saw I in blood. Blood leapt about across the people.
Gerði hríð af hörðu hirð sú er fylkir stýrði.	Made awhile of hordes court-men so were commanded steered.	Made awhile of hordes court-men so were commanding steered.

The Tale of Star-Oddi's Dream (Old Icelandic)

Old Icelandic	Literal	English
Margr er gramr af gengi *göfugr tiginna jöfra.* *Spyrkat eg frægra fyrða* *ferð snjallari verða.* *Þó er gotneskra gumna* *Geirviðr konungr þeira.*	Many were warriors of going noble high-born ruler. Learned I fame among-people journey most-valiant becomes. Though are Gothic men Geirvid the-king theirs.	Many were warriors of going noble high-born rulers. Learned I fame among-people journey most-valiant becomes. And yet of all the Gothic men, Geirvid was their king.
Hlégunnar leit eg hingað *harðráðar ódáðir.* *Ýfð með ylgjar höfði* *eiskranleg réð geisa.* *Trölls kjafta sá eg tyggja* *tönnum hold af mönnum.* *Með hnitgeirum hvofta* *harða sókn of gerði.*	Hlegunn sought I here hard-headed abhorrence. Bristling with wolf's head rage fixed furiously. Trolls jaws saw I chewing teeth the-bodies of men. With battle-spears wafting hard attack with done.	Hlegunn sought I here hard-headed abhorrence bristling with wolf's head rage fixed furiously. Troll's jaws saw I chewing teeth the-bodies of men. With battle-spears wafting a hard attack was done.
Annað sté eg af öðru *Áta skíð um víði* *uns glæsimar Gylfa* *gekk með hilmis rekkum* *og eg siklingi sagðag* *sýslu ægis geisla* *hve grimmhuguð gerði* *Gerðr of vígaferði.*	One stepped I to another Stain wood about wood until gleaming Gylfi went with the-helmsman upright and I the-king told realm Aegir's gleam how grimly done Made too slayings.	I stepped from one to another stained wood about wood until gleaming Gylfi went with the helmsman upright and I told the king the realm of Aegir's gleam how grimly done made too slayings.
Gramr leit hitt hvar hafði *Hörn hvergymis stjörnu* *höfuð á hauka stofni* *heiðingja sér brúðar.* *Ásynju lét elda* *ósvífr konungr hníga* *flóðs af fyllar meiði* *frægr, hinn er ekki vægði.*	Warrior sought to-meet where had Angled each star had upon hawk stem wolf her bride. The-goddesses had flames un-swinging the-king felled flood of full beam far-famed, that was no mercy.	The warrior sought to meet where had each star anged had upon her hawk stem the wolf her bride. The Goddesses had flames unswinging the king felled flood of full beam far-famed, that was no mercy.
Nú er draum þessum lokið er *Stjörnu-Odda dreymdi eftir því* *sem hann sjálfur hefir sagt.*	Now is the-dream this concluded that Star-Oddi dreamed after according as he himself has said.	Now this dream is over that Star-Oddi dreamed according to what he himself has said.

The Tale of Star-Oddi's Dream (Old Icelandic)

Old Icelandic	Literal	English
Og má víst undarlegur og fáheyrður þykja þessi fyrirburður en þó þykir flestum líklegt að hann muni það eina sagt hafa er honum hafi svo þótt verða í drauminum því að Oddi var reiknaður bæði fróður og sannsögull.	And may vision wonder-like and unusual seem this vision but though seems most likely that he would that only told have what he had so thought happened in the-dream because that Oddi was counted both wise and truthful.	And this phenomenon may be considered strange and unheard of, but most people still think that he will have said the only thing that seemed to him to be the case in the dream, because Oddur was considered both knowledgeable and truthful.
Má og ekki undrast þótt kveðskapurinn sé stirður því að í svefni var kveðið.	May also not wonder thought poetry-making being stiff-footed because that in sleep was recited.	It is not surprising that the poetry is stiff because it was recited in sleep.

Word List *(Old Icelandic to English)*

Old Icelandic	English
að	a, in, it, of, so-as, that, the, then, to, with

A, a

Old Icelandic	English
aðra	other
aðrir	others
af	from, of, of, off, to
afla	gain
aflaði	obtained
afli	strength
aftan	aft
aftur	back, returning
albúin	all-prepared
albúinn	all-prepared, all-ready
albúnir	all-prepared
aldregi	never
aldrei	never, never
aldri	age, age
aldurs	of-age, of-age
alla	all, all
allan	all, everything
allfjölmennt	all-many-people
allir	all, all
allóráðlega	all-un-forethought
allra	all, all
allráðlegt	advisable
allri	all
allskyns	all-kinds-of
allt	all, all
allvel	well
alskipuð	fully-prepared
alþýða	the-people
alvopnuðu	all-weaponed
andaður	died
andast	died, died
andskota	enemies
annað	another, one
annaðhvort	another-either, either-way
annan	another, another
annar	one, one, the-other
annarrar	another
annars	anything-else, other, otherwise
arminum	arm
atburð	events
atburður	events, happening
atgervi	deeds
athæfi	behaviour
auðæfum	wealthy-treasures
auði	riches
austr	east
austur	east

Á, á

Old Icelandic	English
á	about, at, by, in, of, on, that, the, then, to, upon
ábyrgð	responsibility
áður	after, before
ágætum	wonderful
ágangi	aggression
áheyrsla	to-hear
ákaflega	extremely
ástir	love, love
ástúð	affection
ástvinum	beloved
ásynju	the-goddesses
áta	stain
átt	have, owned, owned
átta	eight
átti	had
áttu	had
ávallt	always
áverka	injury

Æ, æ

Old Icelandic	English
ægis	Aegir's (name)
ærið	abundance
æsku	youth
ætla	intend

Word List (Old Icelandic to English)

Old Icelandic	English
ætlað	intend
ætt	descendants, lineage
æxti	increased

B, b

Old Icelandic	English
bað	asked, invited
báða	both
báðir	both
báðu	asked
báðum	both
bæði	ask, both
bana	death
bar	bore
barð	ship
bardaga	battle, the-battle
bardagi	battle
bardaginn	the-battle
barmar	brothers
barn	child
barna	child
báru	brought
batnaði	bettering
bauð	offered
beðinn	asking
beiddi	asked
beiðir	demanded
beina	assistance
beitti	biting
bera	borne
berjast	battle, fight
berserkina	berserkers
berserkir	berserkers
berserkjanna	the-berserkers
berserkjunum	the-berserkers
best	best, the-best
besta	best
bestu	best
bestum	best
betur	better
biður	invited
bindur	tied
biti	bit
bjó	lived
blés	blew

Old Icelandic	English
blíðlega	joyfully
blóð	blood
blóðár	bloodied
blóði	blood
blóðísunga	blood-helmeted
böðfrækn	valiant
boði	announced
boðið	invited
böls	spite
borðum	the-tables
borið	bore, brought, carried
borin	brought
börva	trees
brá	drew
bræðir	the-brothers
bragna	heroes
brátt	soon
brattur	broad
braut	away
bregður	reaction
breið	broad
breiðan	wide
brott	away
brúðar	bride
brúðhlaup	the-wedding
brugðnu	drawn
brýtur	subduing
búa	prepare, prepared
búið	preparations, prepared
búins	prepared
bundið	bound
búnir	ready
burt	away
bylgjur	waves
byrjaði	began
byrsóta	windswept

D, d

Old Icelandic	English
dagfinn	Dagfinn (name)
dagfinni	Dagfinn (name)
dagfinnr	Dagfinn (name)
dagfinns	Dagfinn's (name)
dagfinnur	Dagfinn (name)

Word List (Old Icelandic to English)

Old Icelandic	English
daginn	the-day
deili	shared
digran	a-thick
dökkr	dark
dóttur	a-daughter, daughter
draga	drawn
drápa	drapa
drápu	killed
drápuna	drapa
draum	dream, the-dream
drauminn	dream, the-dream
drauminum	the-dream
drengir	warriors
dreymdi	dreamed
dreyra	gore
drjúgt	straight
dró	drew
drótt	people, right
dróttar	right
drottning	the-queen
drottningar	queen, the-queen
drottningin	the-queen
drukkið	drank, drunk
drykk	drink
dvaldist	dwelled
dvelja	dwell
dyggir	virtuous
dyragætti	doorway
dýran	fine
dýrar	precious
dýrðleg	glorious
dýrkuðu	adored
dýrmörum	treasured
dýrra	dear

E, e

Old Icelandic	English
eða	and, or
ef	if
efna	be-carried-out
eftir	after, afterwards
eg	I
eiga	have, only
eigi	none, not
eiginkonu	wife
eignaði	owned
eigu	ownership
eina	only
einkar	very
einkum	especially, particularly
einn	one, only
eins	one
einsætt	evident
einum	one
eiskranleg	rage
eitt	one
eitthvert	some-time
ekki	no, not
elda	flames
eldri	older
ella	either, or-else, otherwise
ellefu	eleven
ellegar	otherwise
en	and, but, however, than, that, the, then, to, what, which
enda	and, with
endemi	unheard-of
engan	no
engi	no, none, not
enn	but, one, that, was
er	am, are, as, for, had, in, is, of, that, the, was, were, what, when, where, which, who
erfð	honoured
erfi	a-toast
erfinu	the-toast
erindi	errand
ert	are
eru	are, they-are, was
eruð	are
eyjarinnar	the-island

F, f

Old Icelandic	English
fá	get, give, marry
faðir	father

Word List (Old Icelandic to English)

Old Icelandic	English
færa	bring
færi	journeyed, means, travel
færu	went
fága	cultivate
fáheyrður	unusual
fái	get
fallin	fallen
fallinn	disposed
fallnir	fallen
fám	few
far	travel
fara	go, to-travel, travel, travelled
farandi	travel
farar	travel
fararinnar	of-the-journey
farast	go
fari	travel
farið	gone, travelling
farmóður	travel-weary
fást	get
fáttkaðist	few
fé	treasure, wealth
fegnir	celebrated
fegurst	fairest
féið	the-treasure
fékk	got
félítill	fee-little
féll	fell
felldi	felled
féllu	fell
fengið	got
fer	it-went, travelled
ferð	journey, the-journey
ferðar	journey, voyage
ferðina	travel, travelling
ferðinni	the-journey
fertug	forty
firrðist	the-firth
fiska	fishing
fjár	wealth
fjárins	wealth
fjarri	far-away
fjölkynngi	sorcery
fjölmenna	many-men
fjölmennan	followers-many
fjölmenni	followers, followers-many, many-followers
flateyjar	Flatey (place)
fleira	more
flestum	most
flóðs	flood
flokkur	flokk
flota	fleet
flutti	brought
föður	father
fólki	folk
föng	possessions, power
fór	did, fared, travelled, went
för	journey, went
forkunnlega	exceedingly
fornum	ancient
fórst	travelled
fóru	going, travel, travelled, went
föruneyti	companionship
föstnuð	betrothed-to
frá	from
frægð	fame
frægr	far-famed
frægra	fame, famous
frægur	famous
frændur	kinsmen
fráfall	death
fram	forwards, from
frama	fame
framast	foremost
frami	courage
frásaga	from-to-say
frásögu	from-saying
fremd	honour
friðaði	peace
fríðust	most-beautiful
fróður	wise
fullgert	full-done
fullkomnir	fully-come
fullt	full
fullu	fully
fund	find, meet

102

Word List (Old Icelandic to English)

Old Icelandic	English
fúsastur	willing
fylgd	follow
fylgi	follows
fylgja	follow
fylgt	followed
fylkir	commanded
fyllar	full
fylltir	filled
fyrða	among-people, fighters
fyrðar	treasure
fyrir	because, before, for
fyrirburð	visions
fyrirburður	vision
fyrr	before
fyrra	first
fyrst	first
fýstu	urged

G, g

Old Icelandic	English
gæfa	good-fortune
gæfu	luck
gaf	gave
gáfu	gave, have
gagn	won
gamall	old
gang	going
ganga	go, going
garp	Garp (name)
garpur	Garp (name)
gata	the-way
gátu	could
gauskrar	of-the-Goths
gauta	of-Goths
gautland	Götaland (place)
gautlandi	Götaland (place)
gautlands	Götaland (place)
gefa	give
gefna	given
geiri	spears
geirvaldr	spear-guardian
geirvið	Geirvid (name)
geirviðar	Geirvid (name)
geirviði	Geirvid (name)
geirviðr	Geirvid (name)
geirviður	Geirvid (name)
geisa	furiously
geisla	gleam
gekk	went
gengi	going
gengið	gone
gengu	went
gengur	went
ger	done, made
gera	be, do, made, to-do
gerði	did, done, made
gerðist	became, begins, came, happened
gerðr	made
gerðu	doing, made
gerðust	made
gersamlega	completely
gerst	done
gert	done, made
gesturinn	the-guest
geta	could, get
getið	told, told-of
geysimikið	exceedingly-great
gift	married
gistingar	guest
gjafvaxta	of-marriage-grown
gjarna	gladly
glaðlega	gladly
glæsimar	gleaming
glögglega	clearly
gný	Gny (name)
gnýr	Gny (name)
góð	good
góðan	good
góðum	good
göfga	noble
göfuglegum	noble-like
göfugr	noble
göndul	Göndul (place)
görva	clearly
gotneskra	Gothic (name)
gott	good
götuna	path
grafinn	the-key
gramr	warrior, warriors

Word List (Old Icelandic to English)

Old Icelandic	English
grams	warriors
greiða	ready
grimmhuguð	grimly
grundu	ground
gullhring	a-gold-ring, gold-ring
gumna	men
gunndjarfr	the-treasurer
gylfa	Gylfi (name)

H, h

Old Icelandic	English
hæglega	comfortable
hætta	conclude
hættlega	dangerously
hæversklega	modestly
hafa	had, have
hafði	had
hafi	had, have
hafiður	raised
hafrastar	eagerly
haft	had
hag	circumstance
halda	hold
hálfs	half
hálsinn	neck
hamingjan	graciousness
hana	her, she
handa	hand, the-hand
handar	hand
hann	he, him, it, to-him
hans	him, his, of-him
hár	high
harða	hard
harðan	hard
harðasti	hardest
harðfengi	toughness
harðráðar	hard-headed
harmaði	mourned
háska	danger
hátt	tall
háttar	kind
haug	a-mound, mound
hauginn	the-mound
hauginum	the-mound
hauka	hawk
haukastóls	hawk-seat
héðan	from-here
hefði	had, have
hefi	have
hefir	had, has, have
hefjast	start
heiðingja	wolf
heilum	whole
heim	home
heima	home
heiman	home
heimkynna	households
heimleiðis	homeward
heimt	drawn
heita	named
heitið	dominion
heitir	named
héldi	held
heldur	rather
helgason	son-of-Helgi (name)
heljarmenn	accursed-men
helju	Hel (place)
helst	rather
hélt	held
hendi	hand
hengiskafla	mound-of-snow
hennar	her, hers
henni	her, hers, she, to-her
her	army
hér	forces, here, she
herðendr	hardy
herför	warfare
herjar	raided
herklæðum	war-clothes
herlíði	war-company
hernað	raiding
hernaði	raiding
herra	lord
hestar	horses
hét	named, was-named
heygður	buried
heyrði	heard
heyrt	heard
hið	the
hildigunnar	Hildigunn (name)

Word List (Old Icelandic to English)

Old Icelandic	English
hildigunnur	Hildigunn (name)
hilmis	helmsman, the-helmsman
hin	the
hina	the, then
hingað	here
hinn	that, the
hinni	the
hins	the
hinum	the, the-others
hirð	court, court-men, retainers
hirðin	courtiers
hirðmaður	court-man
hirðmenn	court-men
hirðmönnum	court-men
hitt	found, to-meet
hittast	meet
hittir	found
hittist	met
hjá	near
hjálmi	the-helm
hjarta	heart
hjó	hewed
hjörgunni	Hjorgunn (name)
hjörgunnur	Hjorgunn (name)
hjörs	sword
hjörvarðar	Hjorvard (name)
hjörvarði	Hjorvard (name)
hjörvarður	Hjorvard (name)
hjuggu	striking
hlaðreið	Hladreid (name)
hlaðreiði	Hladreid (name)
hlégunnar	Hlegunn (name), Hlegunn's (name)
hlégunni	Hlegunn (name)
hlégunnur	Hlegunn (name)
hljóp	ran
hlökk	looking-forward
hlut	lot
hluta	things
hluti	things
hlutum	things
hlýða	listen, obey
hlýddi	followed
hlýra	bows
hneig	strain
hníga	felled
hnigsólar	stricken-sun
hnitgeirum	battle-spears
hóf	began
höfða	headland, Temple-Head (place)
höfðann	headland
höfði	head, headland
höfðingi	chieftain
höfðingja	a-chieftain, chieftains
höfðingjum	chieftains
höfðinglega	nobly
höfðu	had
hofs	temple
hofshöfði	Temple-Head (place)
hófu	had
höfuð	had
höfuðið	head
höfuðin	heads
högg	blows
höggfæri	striking-distance
höggið	the-blow
höggur	struck
hóglegur	comfortably
högna	Hogni's (name)
hold	the-bodies
hóli	hill
hólinn	the-hill
hólinum	the-hill
hóll	hill
hönd	hand
honum	he, him, his, to-him
hörðu	hordes
hörn	angled
horskir	brave
hræ	corpses
hríð	awhile, while
hríðmál	storm
hringa	rings
hringinn	the-ring
hróðbjart	Hrodbjart (name)
hróðbjarti	Hrodbjart (name)
hróðbjarts	Hrodbjart's (name)
hróðbjartur	Hrodbjart (name)
hruðust	cleared

Word List (Old Icelandic to English)

Old Icelandic	English
hug	mind, thought
huga	minds
hugði	thought
hugðu	thought
hugsað	think
hugur	thinking
huldu	covering
hún	her, it, she
hús	house
húsbóndi	housemaster
húsgerðar	house-builder
húsinu	the-house
húss	house
hvað	that, what
hvar	where
hve	how
hver	each, who
hvergi	each
hvergymis	each
hverjum	each
hverra	what
hvers	each
hversu	how-so
hvert	each
hvofta	wafting
hvorir	each
hvorki	neither
hvort	each, either, how
hvortveggja	each-way
hygg	think

I, i

Old Icelandic	English
iðn	crafts
illvirki	outrages
illvirkjanna	for-the-evil-doers, the-evil-doers
illvirkjar	evil-doers
illvirkjarnir	criminals, the-evil-doers
illvirkjunum	evil-doers
inn	in
innan	inside, within

Í, í

Old Icelandic	English
í	about, at, in, of, on, than, the, to
íslandi	Iceland (place)

J, j

Old Icelandic	English
jafnaldra	equal-age
jafnan	always
jafngjarn	equally
jarl	earl, the-earl
jarli	the-earl
jarls	the-earl
jarlsdóttir	the-earl's-daughter
játti	said
jöfra	ruler
jöruskóg	Battle-forest (place)
jöruskógi	Battle-forest (place)
jöruskógur	Battle-forest (place)

K, k

Old Icelandic	English
kæmist	comes
kallaði	claimed
kallaður	called
kann	can, known
kastaði	cast
kaupast	redeem
kaupferðir	merchant-voyages
kempum	champion
kemur	came
kindir	kin
kjafta	jaws
kjöru	chose
kjósa	choices, choose
kjósið	choose
kné	knee
kom	came
koma	came, come
komi	come
komið	came, come
komin	come, coming

Word List (Old Icelandic to English)

Old Icelandic	English
kominn	come
komir	come
komnir	come, coming
komu	came
kómu	came
kona	wife, wife-of, woman
konr	descended
konu	a-wife, wife
konung	the-king
konungdóminn	kingdom
konungi	the-king
konunginn	the-king
konunginum	the-king
konungr	king, the-king
konungs	king, the-king, the-king's
konungsins	the-king, the-king's
konungsmönnum	the-king's-men
konungsskáld	the-king's-poet
konungsskipið	the-king's-ship
konungsskipinu	the-king's-ship
konungssystir	the-king's-sister
konungur	king, the-king
konungurinn	the-king, the-king's, this-king
konur	women
kost	choice
kostaboð	choice-bid
kostað	earned
kosti	benefits
kostir	choose
kostur	choice
kosturinn	choice, distinguished
kunni	know
kunnigt	know, known
kurteislega	courtly
kvað	said, spoke
kvaddi	greeted
kvaðst	said, spoke
kváðu	said
kvæði	announced, a-poem, the-poem
kvæðið	the-poem
kvæðinn	poetry
kvæðinu	the-poem
kvatt	summoned
kveðið	recited
kveðja	called
kveðju	greeting
kveðskapurinn	poetry-making
kveldið	evening
kvenna	the-woman, woman
kvonfang	a-match
kvonfangs	a-match
kvonföngin	a-match
kvongaður	married

L, l

Old Icelandic	English
lá	lay, lying
læst	locked
lágarða	the-surf
lagði	had
lagðist	lay
lagið	granted
lágu	laying-to
land	land
landa	land, lands
landi	land, the-land
landið	land
landinu	the-land
landráða	land-ruling
lands	lands, the-land, the-lands
landsfólkið	the-land's-people
landsfólkinu	lands-folk
landsmönnum	lands-people
landstjórnar	governing
landstjórnin	the-government
langa	long
langar	long
langir	long
langskip	longships
langt	long
láta	allow, allowed, leave, let, lose, to-have
látast	die
latti	discouraged
launa	repay, reward
laust	loosed
laut	place

Word List (Old Icelandic to English)

Old Icelandic	English
leið	company, laid, passes, way
leiðangrs	expedition
leiddi	led
leiðir	led, took
leit	sought
leita	search, searching, seeking
leitaðist	sought
lengi	longer
lengra	longer
lengur	longer
lér	lean
lét	had
letja	discourage
letjast	discouraged
létu	had
létust	had
leyna	concealing
lið	company, crew
liði	company, crew
liðið	passed
liðs	company
liðskosti	provisions
líf	life
lifði	lived
lífi	alive
líflát	life-less
liggja	camped
líka	like
líkaði	liked
líkar	liked
líklegt	likely
list	skills
líta	look, see
lítil	little
lítill	little
lítils	little
litla	little
lítt	a-little, little
ljónar	the-men
ljós	light
ljóslega	lightly
ljótar	hideous
lofsorð	praise
lofuðu	praised

Old Icelandic	English
lögðu	laid
lögðust	camped, laid
lokið	concluded, ended
lönd	the-land
löng	long
losnaði	loosened
löttu	dissuaded
lúka	conclude
luku	unlocked
lygi	lied
lykill	buried
lykka	luck
lyktum	completion
lýsa	show

M, m

Old Icelandic	English
má	may
maður	a-man, man
mælt	spoke, spoken
mælti	spoke
mæltu	spoke
mærði	praise
mætti	may
mættu	may
magni	strength
maki	match
mál	matter
máli	matter, saying, speech, the-matter
málma	words
mann	man, person
mannaðir	mannered
mannaður	brought-up
mannfall	people-felled
mannfallið	people-felling
manni	person
manns	man, man's
mannval	people
margir	many
margr	many
margskonar	many-kinds-of
mart	many
mat	food
mátti	might

Word List (Old Icelandic to English)

Old Icelandic	English
með	between, with
meðan	as-long-as, while
meðr	between
mega	may
megi	may
megin	side, sides
meiði	beam
mein	harm
meir	more
meira	more
meiri	more
menn	men, people
mér	for-me, me, to-me
merkilegasti	remarkable
mest	the-most
mesta	most
mesti	most
mestu	most
mestur	the-greatest
mig	me, myself
mikið	great, greatly, much
mikil	great, much
mikill	much
mikinn	great, much
mikla	much
miklar	much
miklir	great
miklu	great, much
miklum	much
millum	between
mína	my
minna	less
minnar	mine, my
minni	my
minntist	remembered
mínu	my
mínum	mine, my
missa	missed
misst	lost, missed
mitt	mine, my
mjög	most, much
mjög	much
móðir	mother
móður	mother
mönnum	men, people, the-people
morðráð	murder
mörg	many
mörgu	many
morguninn	morning
mörkinni	the-border
mót	meet
móti	meeting
móts	meet
múla	Muli (place)
mun	must, should
mundi	may, remembered, thought, would
mundu	would
muni	should, would
munni	mouth

N, n

Old Icelandic	English
náð	protection
náði	caught
næðist	reached
næmdu	took
nær	near
næst	next
nætur	night
nálega	almost, closely, nearly
nam	took
né	nor
nefnd	named
nefndur	named
nema	except
njóti	appreciate
nokkuð	something, sometime, somewhat
nokkur	someone, something, somewhat
nokkurs	somewhat
norður	in-the-north
nóttina	the-night
nú	how, no, now
nýju	new

O, o

Word List (Old Icelandic to English)

Old Icelandic	English
odda	Oddi (name), Oddi's (name)
oddi	Oddi (name)
of	of, over, too, with
ofan	over
ofangöngunni	over-going
oft	often
og	also, and, of
orð	worded, words
orða	words
orðahjaldur	word-struggle
orðin	become
orðinn	become
orku	power
ort	worded
orustu	battle
orustunni	the-battle
oss	us

Ó, ó

Old Icelandic	English
óboðið	uninvited
ódáðir	abhorrence
ódælli	un-pleasant
ógrynni	mass
óhægindi	inconvenience
ójafnað	unequal
ójafnari	unequal
ólát	un-courteous
ósnöfurmannlega	un-alert
ósvífr	un-swinging

Ö, ö

Old Icelandic	English
öðru	another, others
öðrum	another, each-other, to-other
öfúsa	gratitude
öllu	all
öllum	all, of-all
önnur	others

P, p

Old Icelandic	English
presentur	presents
prúðlegsta	most-prolific
prýði	finery

R, r

Old Icelandic	English
ráð	advice, decide, decision, statements
ráða	prevail
ráðahag	marriage, marriage-proposal
ráðast	arrange, arranging
ráði	conduct, consent, decision
ráðist	determine
ráðlegt	advice
ráðvandur	honest
ræðst	decided
rammgert	firmly-built
rammlega	firmly
raunar	actually
réð	fixed, ruled, ruling
réðst	had
réðust	appointed
reiknaður	counted
rekka	unfolded
rekkju	bed
rekkum	upright
reykjardal	Reykjardal (place)
reyna	test
riðu	rode
ríkar	rich
ríki	kingdom, the-kingdom
ríkið	the-kingdom
ríkinu	the-kingdom
ríkis	kingdom, the-kingdom
ríkisstjórnar	governor
ríkustum	kingdom's
rímkænn	calendar-computation-wise
ritnar	written
rjóður	clearing

Word List (Old Icelandic to English)

Old Icelandic	English
roðbjartssonr	Son-of-Hrodbjart (name)
rómu	a-roar, battle

S, s

Old Icelandic	English
sá	saw, seen, so, that
sæju	saw
sækja	seek, sought
sæma	honour, the-same
sæmd	honour
sæmdi	honour
sæmilegar	honourable
safnað	gathered
safnar	gathered
sagan	the-saga
sagðag	told
sagði	said, telling, the-saga, told, told
sagðist	said
sagt	said, said, told
sakir	for-the-sake-of, sake, the-sake-of
sama	same
saman	the-same, together
sameignar	fight, the-fight
samfarar	interaction
samför	together, togetherness
samtíða	contemporary
sannsögull	truthful
sárum	wounds
sat	sat
satt	the-truth
sáu	saw
sé	being
séð	seen
seggir	said
seggja	say
seggjum	men
segir	said
segja	said, say
seglhættu	sail-danger
seldur	sold
sem	as, so, that, was, which
sén	seen
sendi	sent
sendimenn	messengers, sending-men
sendir	sent
sér	as, he, her, herself, himself, his, themselves
sért	are
sett	sat, set
settan	appointed
setti	set
settur	sat, set
setur	set
séu	are
sið	customs, traditions
síðan	after, afterwards, then
síðar	afterwards
síðara	latter
sig	herself, himself, his, themselves
sigldum	we-sailed
siglu	sail
sigrgöfgaðir	victory-gift-gods
sigri	victory
sigur	victory
siklingi	the-king
siklingr	the-king
siklings	the-king's
síldasund	Herring-sound (place)
síldasundi	Herring-sound (place)
sín	her, his, their
sína	himself, his
sinn	her, hers, his, one-day
sinna	their
sinni	hers, his, times
síns	his
sínu	her, his
sínum	hers, theirs
sitja	sit
sitt	his, their
sjá	look, saw, see, so
sjái	see

Word List (Old Icelandic to English)

Old Icelandic	English	Old Icelandic	English
sjáir	look	*skóg*	forest
sjálf	herself	*skóginn*	the-forest
sjálfum	himself, yourself	*skör*	across
sjálfur	himself	*skorta*	shortage
sjár	the-sea	*skorti*	shortage
sjást	t-look	*skóþvenginn*	shoe-thong
skaði	harm	*skóþvengur*	shoe-thong
skafti	spear	*skreið*	glided
skal	shall	*skríða*	action
skáld	poet, the-poet	*skuluð*	should
skáldi	the-poet	*skyldari*	obliged
skáldinu	the-poet	*skyldi*	should
skálds	the-poet	*skyldu*	should
skáldskaparlaunum	poet's-reward	*skynda*	hurrying
skeið	sheathed-sword	*slíka*	such
skemmtanar	entertainment	*slíks*	such
skemur	shorter	*slíku*	so, such
skerðendr	diminished	*slíkum*	such
skíð	wood	*smágrjót*	small-stones
skildi	shield, should	*snarpir*	sharply
skildu	knew	*snarpri*	rough, roughly
skiljast	separate	*snarráðir*	quickly
skilnaður	parting	*snemma*	soon
skip	ships	*snjallari*	most-valiant
skipaferðum	ship's-course	*snýr*	turned
skipaflota	ship-fleet	*sofnaði*	slept
skipaflotann	ship-fleet	*sofnar*	slept
skipan	the-ship	*sögðu*	said
skipanna	the-ships	*sögu*	telling
skipi	the-ship	*söguna*	the-saga
skips	the-ships	*sögunnar*	the-saga
skipstjórnarmaður	ship-steering-man	*sögunni*	the-saga
skipta	divide, exchange	*sókn*	attack, attacked
skipti	exchanged	*sóma*	honour
skiptum	exchanged	*sómasamlegri*	respectable
skipuð	prepared	*sómi*	honour
skjaldmær	shield-maiden	*son*	son
skjaldmeyja	shield-maidens	*sonar*	son
skjaldmeyjar	shield-maidens	*sótt*	attended, sickness
skjóma	shimmering	*sótti*	attended, attending, encountered
skjót	launched		
skjóta	short, throw	*sóttin*	sickness
skjótara	shorter	*sóttu*	attended
skjótast	quickly, soonest	*spurði*	asked
skjótt	quickly	*spyrjast*	was-heard
		spyrkat	learned

Word List (Old Icelandic to English)

Old Icelandic	English	*Old Icelandic*	English
stað	place	*svipan*	swooping
staddir	standing	*svívirðing*	disgraceful
staddur	placed, stood	*svo*	so, such, to
staði	places	*sýndist*	seemed
staðið	placed, stood	*sýnist*	seems
standa	standing	*sýslu*	realm
sté	stepped	*sýslumenn*	stewards
steig	leapt	*systir*	sister
sterkur	strong		
stíg	path		
stigamannanna	the-robbing-men		
stigamönnunum	the-robbers		

T, t

Old Icelandic	English
stígur	climbed
stirður	stiff-footed
stjórn	control
stjórna	ruling
stjörnu	star
stjörnum	the-stars
stjörnu-odda	Star-Oddi (name)
stjörnu-oddi	Star-Oddi (name)
stjörnur	stars
stóð	place, stood
stóðu	stood
stofnað	planned
stofni	stem
stökk	leapt
stól	throne
stór	great
stóra	great
stórmannlega	great-man-like
stórum	great
stund	awhile
stýrði	guided, steered
sú	so, this
sumir	some
sund	a-sound
sundin	the-sound
sundunum	sound, the-sound
svarar	answer, answered
svari	answer
svefni	sleep
sverða	swords
sverði	sword
sverðinu	sword
svikmenni	the-wicked

Old Icelandic	English
taka	take, taken
takast	take, took
talað	told
talar	speak
taldi	said
tekinn	taken
tekst	takes
tekur	took
tíðinda	news
tíðindi	news, the-news
tíðindin	news
tíðindum	news
tiginna	high-born
tign	prestige
tignar	princely
til	for, that, to
tilföngum	means
tíma	time
tímar	time
tindótt	toothed
tírgjarn	fame-ambition
tíska	fashion
títt	report
tjáð	expressed
tjóa	avail
tók	took
tókust	took
töldu	told
tólf	twelve
tönnum	teeth
treysta	trust
trölls	trolls
tröllslegt	trollish
tryggðarmaður	faithful-man

Word List (Old Icelandic to English)

Old Icelandic	English
tugum	tens
tveggja	two
tveir	two
tvo	two
tyggja	chewing

Þ, þ

Old Icelandic	English
þá	then
það	it, that, the, then, they, this, to
þaðan	from-there, then
þær	they
þætti	seemed, thought
þakkaði	thanked
þakkar	thanked
þangað	from-there, there
þangi	seaweed
þann	that, then
þar	of, that, then, there, they
þarf	needed
þau	the, there, they
þegar	as-soon-as, immediately, straightaway, they
þegnum	subjects
þeim	them, they
þeir	them, there, they
þeira	theirs
þeiri	there
þeirra	of-them, their, theirs, them, there, they
þeirri	that
þenna	these, this
þér	to-you, you
þess	it, the, this
þessa	of-this, these, this
þessar	these, this
þessarar	this
þessari	this
þessi	the, these, this
þessir	these
þessu	this
þessum	this
þetta	that, the, this
þig	you
þiggja	accept
þín	yours
þing	assembly, the-assembly
þingað	assembled
þings	an-assembly, assembly
þjóða	people
þjóðar	great-river, king
þjóðbrautinni	the-highway
þó	though, yet
Þórður	Thord (name)
þótt	though, thought
þótti	seemed, thought
þóttist	seemed, though, thought
þóttust	thought
þraut	finished
þrekvirki	brave-deeds
þriðjung	a-third-of
þrítug	thirty
þrjú	three
þroskast	develop
þú	you
þurfa	needed
þurfti	need
þustu	flailing
þvenginn	thong
því	according, accordingly, according-to, against, because, for, then, therefore
þvílíks	such-like
þyki	thought
þykir	seemed, seems
þykja	regarded, seem

U, u

Old Icelandic	English
um	about
umbúnaður	soft-bed-prepared
ummæli	about-words
umsjá	supervision

Word List (Old Icelandic to English)

Old Icelandic	English
und	under
undan	under
undarlegt	wonder-like
undarlegur	extraordinary, wonder-like
undir	under
undrast	wonder
undur	wonder
ung	young
unga	young
ungur	young
unna	grant, love
uns	ours, until
upp	up
upphaf	beginning
upphafi	became
uppheldi	advancement
urðu	became
utan	without

Ú, ú

Old Icelandic	English
úr	from, out-of, through, with
út	out, out-from
útbyrðis	overboard
úti	out
útilegumannanna	the-outlaw-men

V, v

Old Icelandic	English
vægði	mercy
vægis	weight
vænn	handsome
væri	being, was, were, would-be
vág	inlet
vaknað	woken
vaknaði	awoke, woke
vakni	wake
vald	power
valda	wield
vandræði	difficulty
vanir	friends
vantaði	lacking
vanur	accustomed
var	was, were
varð	became, was
varfærir	caution
varp	thrown
vaxa	grow
vaxið	grown
véar	the-gods
veðri	the-weather
veg	way
vega	ways
vegg	wall
veglegasta	greatest
vegs	glory
veisla	feast
veislu	feast
veisluna	feast, the-feast
veislunni	the-feast
veit	know
veitt	given
veitti	gave
veittur	given
vel	all, well
velja	choose
venja	way
venju	habitually
vera	be, being, was
verða	be, become, becomes, happened, to-be, worthy
verði	be
verður	became, worth
verið	been
verkmaður	working-man
vetra	winters
vexti	grown
við	against, with
víða	wide, widely, with
viðbúnaði	preparation
víði	wood
viður	trees
vígaferði	slayings
vígboði	battle-bidding
vígroða	warfare
vigrum	spears

Word List (Old Icelandic to English)

Old Icelandic	English
víking	viking, viking-raids
víkinga	vikings
víkingar	vikings
vil	will, wish
vildi	willed, wished
vildu	willed, wished
vilja	willed
vilji	wish
viljið	wish
vill	wanted-to, will, wish
viltu	will-you
vinir	friends
vinna	grant
vinstri	left
vinum	friends
virðar	men
virðing	worth, worthiness, worthy
virðingu	worthiness
virðulega	worthily
virðulegri	worthy
virðulegur	worthy
virktamönnum	chosen-man
virktavinum	friends
vís	aware
vísaði	pointed-out
vísir	know
vissi	knew
vist	hospitality
víst	vision
vísur	verse, verses
vit	to
vita	knew, know, to-know
vitja	visit
vitmikill	knowing-much
vitrasta	wisest
vitrustum	wise
vitur	wise
vó	guarded
vöknuðu	awoke
von	expected, expected, expecting
vopnaðir	weaponed
vopnaskipti	weapons-exchange
vopnfimi	weapon-nimble
vopnum	weapons

Old Icelandic	English
vor	our
vörn	defended
vorrar	aware
voru	they-were, was, were, were

Y, y

yður	of-you, to-you, you
yðvarrar	your
yðvarri	your
yfir	over
yfirkoma	overcome
ylgjar	wolf's
ylgjarhöfuð	she-wolf's-head
yrði	became

Ý, ý

ýfð	bristling
ýmissa	various

Word List *(English to Old Icelandic)*

English / *Old Icelandic*

A, a

English	Old Icelandic
a	*að*
abhorrence	*ódáðir*
about	*á, í, um*
about-words	*ummæli*
abundance	*ærið*
accept	*þiggja*
according	*því*
accordingly	*því*
according-to	*því*
accursed-men	*heljarmenn*
accustomed	*vanur*
a-chieftain	*höfðingja*
across	*skör*
action	*skríða*
actually	*raunar*
a-daughter	*dóttur*
adored	*dýrkuðu*
advancement	*uppheldi*
advice	*ráð, ráðlegt*
advisable	*allráðlegt*
Aegir's (name)	*ægis*
affection	*ástúð*
aft	*aftan*
after	*áður, eftir, síðan*
afterwards	*eftir, síðan, síðar*
against	*því, við*
age	*aldri*
aggression	*ágangi*
a-gold-ring	*gullhring*
a-little	*lítt*
alive	*lífi*
all	*alla, allan, allir, allra, allri, allt, öllu, öllum, vel*
all-kinds-of	*allskyns*
all-many-people	*allfjölmennt*
allow	*láta*
allowed	*láta*
all-prepared	*albúin, albúinn, albúnir*
all-ready	*albúinn*
all-un-forethought	*allóráðlega*
all-weaponed	*alvopnuðu*
almost	*nálega*
also	*og*
always	*ávallt, jafnan*
am	*er*
a-man	*maður*
a-match	*kvonfang, kvonfangs, kvonföngin*
among-people	*fyrða*
a-mound	*haug*
an-assembly	*þings*
ancient	*fornum*
and	*eða, en, enda, og*
angled	*hörn*
announced	*boði, kvæði*
another	*annað, annan, annarrar, öðru, öðrum*
another-either	*annaðhvort*
answer	*svarar, svari*
answered	*svarar*
anything-else	*annars*
a-poem	*kvæði*
appointed	*réðust, settan*
appreciate	*njóti*
are	*er, ert, eru, eruð, sért, séu*
arm	*arminum*
army	*her*
a-roar	*rómu*
arrange	*ráðast*
arranging	*ráðast*
as	*er, sem, sér*
ask	*bæði*
asked	*bað, báðu, beiddi, spurði*
asking	*beðinn*
as-long-as	*meðan*
a-sound	*sund*
assembled	*þingað*
assembly	*þing, þings*
assistance	*beina*

Word List (English to Old Icelandic)

English	Old Icelandic
as-soon-as	þegar
at	á, í
a-thick	digran
a-third-of	þriðjung
a-toast	erfi
attack	sókn
attacked	sókn
attended	sótt, sótti, sóttu
attending	sótti
avail	tjóa
aware	vís, vorrar
away	braut, brott, burt
awhile	hríð, stund
a-wife	konu
awoke	vaknaði, vöknuðu

B, b

English	Old Icelandic
back	aftur
battle	bardaga, bardagi, berjast, orustu, rómu
battle-bidding	vígboði
Battle-forest (place)	jöruskóg, jöruskógi, jöruskógur
battle-spears	hnitgeirum
be	gera, vera, verða, verði
beam	meiði
became	gerðist, upphafi, urðu, varð, verður, yrði
be-carried-out	efna
because	fyrir, því
become	orðin, orðinn, verða
becomes	verða
bed	rekkju
been	verið
before	áður, fyrir, fyrr
began	byrjaði, hóf
beginning	upphaf
begins	gerðist
behaviour	athæfi
being	sé, væri, vera
beloved	ástvinum
benefits	kosti
berserkers	berserkina, berserkir
best	best, besta, bestu, bestum
betrothed-to	föstnuð
better	betur
bettering	batnaði
between	með, meðr, millum
bit	biti
biting	beitti
blew	blés
blood	blóð, blóði
blood-helmeted	blóðísunga
bloodied	blóðár
blows	högg
bore	bar, borið
borne	bera
both	báða, báðir, báðum, bæði
bound	bundið
bows	hlýra
brave	horskir
brave-deeds	þrekvirki
bride	brúðar
bring	færa
bristling	ýfð
broad	brattur, breið
brothers	barmar
brought	báru, borið, borin, flutti
brought-up	mannaður
buried	heygður, lykill
but	en, enn
by	á

C, c

English	Old Icelandic
calendar-computation-wise	rímkænn
called	kallaður, kveðja
came	gerðist, kemur, kom, koma, komið, komu, kómu
camped	liggja, lögðust
can	kann
carried	borið
cast	kastaði
caught	náði

Word List (English to Old Icelandic)

English	*Old Icelandic*	English	*Old Icelandic*
caution	*varfærir*	courtly	*kurteislega*
celebrated	*fegnir*	court-man	*hirðmaður*
champion	*kempum*	court-men	*hirð, hirðmenn, hirðmönnum*
chewing	*tyggja*		
chieftain	*höfðingi*	covering	*huldu*
chieftains	*höfðingja, höfðingjum*	crafts	*iðn*
child	*barn, barna*	crew	*lið, liði*
choice	*kost, kostur, kosturinn*	criminals	*illvirkjarnir*
choice-bid	*kostaboð*	cultivate	*fága*
choices	*kjósa*	customs	*sið*
choose	*kjósa, kjósið, kostir, velja*		
chose	*kjöru*		

D, d

English	*Old Icelandic*
chosen-man	*virktamönnum*
circumstance	*hag*
claimed	*kallaði*
cleared	*hruðust*
clearing	*rjóður*
clearly	*glögglega, görva*
climbed	*stígur*
closely	*nálega*
come	*koma, komi, komið, komin, kominn, komir, komnir*
comes	*kæmist*
comfortable	*hæglega*
comfortably	*hóglegur*
coming	*komin, komnir*
commanded	*fylkir*
companionship	*föruneyti*
company	*leið, lið, liði, liðs*
completely	*gersamlega*
completion	*lyktum*
concealing	*leyna*
conclude	*hætta, lúka*
concluded	*lokið*
conduct	*ráði*
consent	*ráði*
contemporary	*samtíða*
control	*stjórn*
corpses	*hræ*
could	*gátu, geta*
counted	*reiknaður*
courage	*frami*
court	*hirð*
courtiers	*hirðin*

English	*Old Icelandic*
Dagfinn (name)	*dagfinn, dagfinni, dagfinnr, dagfinnur*
Dagfinn's (name)	*dagfinns*
danger	*háska*
dangerously	*hættlega*
dark	*dökkr*
daughter	*dóttur*
dear	*dýrra*
death	*bana, fráfall*
decide	*ráð*
decided	*ræðst*
decision	*ráð, ráði*
deeds	*atgervi*
defended	*vörn*
demanded	*beiðir*
descendants	*ætt*
descended	*konr*
determine	*ráðist*
develop	*þroskast*
did	*fór, gerði*
die	*látast*
died	*andaður, andast*
difficulty	*vandræði*
diminished	*skerðendr*
discourage	*letja*
discouraged	*latti, letjast*
disgraceful	*svívirðing*
disposed	*fallinn*
dissuaded	*löttu*
distinguished	*kosturinn*
divide	*skipta*
do	*gera*

Word List (English to Old Icelandic)

English	*Old Icelandic*	English	*Old Icelandic*
doing	*gerðu*	exceedingly-great	*geysimikið*
dominion	*heitið*	except	*nema*
done	*ger, gerði, gerst, gert*	exchange	*skipta*
doorway	*dyragætti*	exchanged	*skipti, skiptum*
drank	*drukkið*	expected	*von*
drapa	*drápa, drápuna*	expecting	*von*
drawn	*brugðnu, draga, heimt*	expedition	*leiðangrs*
dream	*draum, drauminn*	expressed	*tjáð*
dreamed	*dreymdi*	extraordinary	*undarlegur*
drew	*brá, dró*	extremely	*ákaflega*
drink	*drykk*		
drunk	*drukkið*		
dwell	*dvelja*		
dwelled	*dvaldist*		

E, e

F, f

English	*Old Icelandic*
each	*hver, hvergi, hvergymis, hverjum, hvers, hvert, hvorir, hvort*
each-other	*öðrum*
each-way	*hvortveggja*
eagerly	*hafrastar*
earl	*jarl*
earned	*kostað*
east	*austr, austur*
eight	*átta*
either	*ella, hvort*
either-way	*annaðhvort*
eleven	*ellefu*
encountered	*sótti*
ended	*lokið*
enemies	*andskota*
entertainment	*skemmtanar*
equal-age	*jafnaldra*
equally	*jafngjarn*
errand	*erindi*
especially	*einkum*
evening	*kveldið*
events	*atburð, atburður*
everything	*allan*
evident	*einsætt*
evil-doers	*illvirkjar, illvirkjunum*
exceedingly	*forkunnlega*

English	*Old Icelandic*
fairest	*fegurst*
faithful-man	*tryggðarmaður*
fallen	*fallin, fallnir*
fame	*frægð, frægra, frama*
fame-ambition	*tírgjarn*
famous	*frægra, frægur*
far-away	*fjarri*
fared	*fór*
far-famed	*frægr*
fashion	*tíska*
father	*faðir, föður*
feast	*veisla, veislu, veisluna*
fee-little	*félítill*
fell	*féll, féllu*
felled	*felldi, hníga*
few	*fám, fáttkaðist*
fight	*berjast, sameignar*
fighters	*fyrða*
filled	*fylltir*
find	*fund*
fine	*dýran*
finery	*prýði*
finished	*þraut*
firmly	*rammlega*
firmly-built	*rammgert*
first	*fyrra, fyrst*
fishing	*fiska*
fixed	*réð*
flailing	*þustu*
flames	*elda*
Flatey (place)	*flateyjar*

Word List (English to Old Icelandic)

English	Old Icelandic	English	Old Icelandic
fleet	flota	given	gefna, veitt, veittur
flokk	flokkur	gladly	gjarna, glaðlega
flood	flóðs	gleam	geisla
folk	fólki	gleaming	glæsimar
follow	fylgd, fylgja	glided	skreið
followed	fylgt, hlýddi	glorious	dýrðleg
followers	fjölmenni	glory	vegs
followers-many	fjölmennan, fjölmenni	Gny (name)	gný, gnýr
follows	fylgi	go	fara, farast, ganga
food	mat	going	fóru, gang, ganga, gengi
for	er, fyrir, því, til	gold-ring	gullhring
forces	hér	Göndul (place)	göndul
foremost	framast	gone	farið, gengið
forest	skóg	good	góð, góðan, góðum, gott
for-me	mér	good-fortune	gæfa
for-the-evil-doers	illvirkjanna	gore	dreyra
for-the-sake-of	sakir	got	fékk, fengið
forty	fertug	Götaland (place)	gautland, gautlandi, gautlands
forwards	fram	Gothic (name)	gotneskra
found	hitt, hittir	governing	landstjórnar
friends	vanir, vinir, vinum, virktavinum	governor	ríkisstjórnar
from	af, frá, fram, úr	graciousness	hamingjan
from-here	héðan	grant	unna, vinna
from-saying	frásögu	granted	lagið
from-there	þaðan, þangað	gratitude	öfúsa
from-to-say	frásaga	great	mikið, mikil, mikinn, miklir, miklu, stór, stóra, stórum
full	fullt, fyllar	greatest	veglegasta
full-done	fullgert	greatly	mikið
fully	fullu	great-man-like	stórmannlega
fully-come	fullkomnir	great-river	þjóðar
fully-prepared	alskipuð	greeted	kvaddi
furiously	geisa	greeting	kveðju
		grimly	grimmhuguð

G, g

English	Old Icelandic	English	Old Icelandic
gain	afla	ground	grundu
Garp (name)	garp, garpur	grow	vaxa
gathered	safnað, safnar	grown	vaxið, vexti
gave	gaf, gáfu, veitti	guarded	vó
Geirvid (name)	geirvið, geirviðar, geirviði, geirviðr, geirviður	guest	gistingar
get	fá, fái, fást, geta	guided	stýrði
give	fá, gefa	Gylfi (name)	gylfa

Word List (English to Old Icelandic)

English	*Old Icelandic*	English	*Old Icelandic*
		Hildigunn (name)	*hildigunnar, hildigunnur*
H, h		hill	*hóli, hóll*
habitually	*venju*	him	*hann, hans, honum*
had	*átti, áttu, er, hafa, hafði, hafi, haft, hefði, hefir, höfðu, hófu, höfuð, lagði, lét, létu, létust, réðst*	himself	*sér, sig, sína, sjálfum, sjálfur*
		his	*hans, honum, sér, sig, sín, sína, sinn, sinni, síns, sínu, sitt*
half	*hálfs*	Hjorgunn (name)	*hjörgunni, hjörgunnur*
hand	*handa, handar, hendi, hönd*	Hjorvard (name)	*hjörvarðar, hjörvarði, hjörvarður*
handsome	*vænn*	Hladreid (name)	*hlaðreið, hlaðreiði*
happened	*gerðist, verða*	Hlegunn (name)	*hlégunnar, hlégunni, hlégunnur*
happening	*atburður*		
hard	*harða, harðan*	Hlegunn's (name)	*hlégunnar*
hardest	*harðasti*	Hogni's (name)	*högna*
hard-headed	*harðráðar*	hold	*halda*
hardy	*herðendr*	home	*heim, heima, heiman*
harm	*mein, skaði*	homeward	*heimleiðis*
has	*hefir*	honest	*ráðvandur*
have	*átt, eiga, gáfu, hafa, hafi, hefði, hefi, hefir*	honour	*fremd, sæma, sæmd, sæmdi, sóma, sómi*
hawk	*hauka*	honourable	*sæmilegar*
hawk-seat	*haukastóls*	honoured	*erfð*
he	*hann, honum, sér*	hordes	*hörðu*
head	*höfði, höfuðið*	horses	*hestar*
headland	*höfða, höfðann, höfði*	hospitality	*vist*
heads	*höfuðin*	house	*hús, húss*
heard	*heyrði, heyrt*	house-builder	*húsgerðar*
heart	*hjarta*	households	*heimkynna*
Hel (place)	*helju*	housemaster	*húsbóndi*
held	*héldi, hélt*	how	*hve, hvort, nú*
helmsman	*hilmis*	however	*en*
her	*hana, hennar, henni, hún, sér, sín, sinn, sínu*	how-so	*hversu*
		Hrodbjart (name)	*hróðbjart, hróðbjarti, hróðbjartur*
here	*hér, hingað*	Hrodbjart's (name)	*hróðbjarts*
heroes	*bragna*	hurrying	*skynda*
Herring-sound (place)	*síldasund, síldasundi*		
hers	*hennar, henni, sinn, sinni, sínum*	**I, i**	
herself	*sér, sig, sjálf*		
hewed	*hjó*	I	*eg*
hideous	*ljótar*	Iceland (place)	*íslandi*
high	*hár*	if	*ef*
high-born	*tiginna*	immediately	*þegar*

Word List (English to Old Icelandic)

English	Old Icelandic
in	*á, að, er, í, inn*
inconvenience	*óhægindi*
increased	*æxti*
injury	*áverka*
inlet	*vág*
inside	*innan*
intend	*ætla, ætlað*
interaction	*samfarar*
in-the-north	*norður*
invited	*bað, biður, boðið*
is	*er*
it	*að, hann, hún, það, þess*
it-went	*fer*

J, j

jaws	*kjafta*
journey	*ferð, ferðar, för*
journeyed	*færi*
joyfully	*blíðlega*

K, k

killed	*drápu*
kin	*kindir*
kind	*háttar*
king	*konungr, konungs, konungur, þjóðar*
kingdom	*konungdóminn, ríki, ríkis*
kingdom's	*ríkustum*
kinsmen	*frændur*
knee	*kné*
knew	*skildu, vissi, vita*
know	*kunni, kunnigt, veit, vísir, vita*
knowing-much	*vitmikill*
known	*kann, kunnigt*

L, l

lacking	*vantaði*
laid	*leið, lögðu, lögðust*
land	*land, landa, landi, landið*
land-ruling	*landráða*
lands	*landa, lands*
lands-folk	*landsfólkinu*
lands-people	*landsmönnum*
latter	*síðara*
launched	*skjót*
lay	*lá, lagðist*
laying-to	*lágu*
lean	*lér*
leapt	*steig, stökk*
learned	*spyrkat*
leave	*láta*
led	*leiddi, leiðir*
left	*vinstri*
less	*minna*
let	*láta*
lied	*lygi*
life	*líf*
life-less	*líflát*
light	*ljós*
lightly	*ljóslega*
like	*líka*
liked	*líkaðl, líkar*
likely	*líklegt*
lineage	*ætt*
listen	*hlýða*
little	*lítil, lítill, lítils, litla, lítt*
lived	*bjó, lifði*
locked	*læst*
long	*langa, langar, langir, langt, löng*
longer	*lengi, lengra, lengur*
longships	*langskip*
look	*líta, sjá, sjáir*
looking-forward	*hlökk*
loosed	*laust*
loosened	*losnaði*
lord	*herra*
lose	*láta*
lost	*misst*
lot	*hlut*
love	*ástir, unna*
luck	*gæfu, lykka*
lying	*lá*

Word List (English to Old Icelandic)

English	Old Icelandic

M, m

English	Old Icelandic
made	ger, gera, gerði, gerðr, gerðu, gerðust, gert
man	maður, mann, manns
mannered	mannaðir
man's	manns
many	margir, margr, mart, mörg, mörgu
many-followers	fjölmenni
many-kinds-of	margskonar
many-men	fjölmenna
marriage	ráðahag
marriage-proposal	ráðahag
married	gift, kvongaður
marry	fá
mass	ógrynni
match	maki
matter	mál, máli
may	má, mætti, mættu, mega, megi, mundi
me	mér, mig
means	færi, tilföngum
meet	fund, hittast, mót, móts
meeting	móti
men	gumna, menn, mönnum, seggjum, virðar
merchant-voyages	kaupferðir
mercy	vægði
messengers	sendimenn
met	hittist
might	mátti
mind	hug
minds	huga
mine	minnar, mínum, mitt
missed	missa, misst
modestly	hæversklega
more	fleira, meir, meira, meiri
morning	morguninn
most	flestum, mesta, mesti, mestu, mjög
most-beautiful	fríðust
most-prolific	prúðlegsta
most-valiant	snjallari
mother	móðir, móður
mound	haug
mound-of-snow	hengiskafla
mourned	harmaði
mouth	munni
much	mikið, mikil, mikill, mikinn, mikla, miklar, miklu, miklum, mjög, mjög
Muli (place)	múla
murder	morðráð
must	mun
my	mína, minnar, minni, mínu, mínum, mitt
myself	mig

N, n

English	Old Icelandic
named	heita, heitir, hét, nefnd, nefndur
near	hjá, nær
nearly	nálega
neck	hálsinn
need	þurfti
needed	þarf, þurfa
neither	hvorki
never	aldregi, aldrei
new	nýju
news	tíðinda, tíðindi, tíðindin, tíðindum
next	næst
night	nætur
no	ekki, engan, engi, nú
noble	göfga, göfugr
noble-like	göfuglegum
nobly	höfðinglega
none	eigi, engi
nor	né
not	eigi, ekki, engi
now	nú

O, o

Word List (English to Old Icelandic)

English	Old Icelandic	English	Old Icelandic
obey	hlýða		
obliged	skyldari		
obtained	aflaði		
Oddi (name)	odda, oddi		
Oddi's (name)	odda		
of	á, að, af, er, í, of, og, þar		
of-age	aldurs		
of-all	öllum		
off	af		
offered	bauð		
of-Goths	gauta		
of-him	hans		
of-marriage-grown	gjafvaxta		
often	oft		
of-the-Goths	gauskrar		
of-the-journey	fararinnar		
of-them	þeirra		
of-this	þessa		
of-you	yður		
old	gamall		
older	eldri		
on	á, í		
one	annað, annar, einn, eins, einum, eitt, enn		
one-day	sinn		
only	eiga, eina, einn		
or	eða		
or-else	ella		
other	aðra, annars		
others	aðrir, öðru, önnur		
otherwise	annars, ella, ellegar		
our	vor		
ours	uns		
out	út, úti		
out-from	út		
out-of	úr		
outrages	illvirki		
over	of, ofan, yfir		
overboard	útbyrðis		
overcome	yfirkoma		
over-going	ofangöngunni		
owned	átt, eignaði		
ownership	eigu		

P, p

English	Old Icelandic
particularly	einkum
parting	skilnaður
passed	liðið
passes	leið
path	götuna, stíg
peace	friðaði
people	drótt, mannval, menn, mönnum, þjóða
people-felled	mannfall
people-felling	mannfallið
person	mann, manni
place	laut, stað, stóð
placed	staddur, staðið
places	staði
planned	stofnað
poet	skáld
poetry	kvæðinn
poetry-making	kveðskapurinn
poet's-reward	skáldskaparlaunum
pointed-out	vísaði
possessions	föng
power	föng, orku, vald
praise	lofsorð, mærði
praised	lofuðu
precious	dýrar
preparation	viðbúnaði
preparations	búið
prepare	búa
prepared	búa, búið, búins, skipuð
presents	presentur
prestige	tign
prevail	ráða
princely	tignar
protection	náð
provisions	liðskosti

Q, q

English	Old Icelandic
queen	drottningar
quickly	skjótast, skjótt, snarráðir

Word List (English to Old Icelandic)

English	*Old Icelandic*

R, r

English	*Old Icelandic*
rage	*eiskranleg*
raided	*herjar*
raiding	*hernað, hernaði*
raised	*hafiður*
ran	*hljóp*
rather	*heldur, helst*
reached	*næðist*
reaction	*bregður*
ready	*búnir, greiða*
realm	*sýslu*
recited	*kveðið*
redeem	*kaupast*
regarded	*þykja*
remarkable	*merkilegasti*
remembered	*minntist, mundi*
repay	*launa*
report	*títt*
respectable	*sómasamlegri*
responsibility	*ábyrgð*
retainers	*hirð*
returning	*aftur*
reward	*launa*
Reykjardal (place)	*reykjardal*
rich	*ríkar*
riches	*auði*
right	*drótt, dróttar*
rings	*hringa*
rode	*riðu*
rough	*snarpri*
roughly	*snarpri*
ruled	*réð*
ruler	*jöfra*
ruling	*réð, stjórna*

S, s

English	*Old Icelandic*
said	*játti, kvað, kvaðst, kváðu, sagði, sagðist, sagt, seggir, segir, segja, sögðu, taldi*
sail	*siglu*
sail-danger	*seglhættu*
sake	*sakir*
same	*sama*
sat	*sat, sett, settur*
saw	*sá, sæju, sáu, sjá*
say	*seggja, segja*
saying	*máli*
search	*leita*
searching	*leita*
seaweed	*þangi*
see	*líta, sjá, sjái*
seek	*sækja*
seeking	*leita*
seem	*þykja*
seemed	*sýndist, bætti, þótti, þóttist, þykir*
seems	*sýnist, þykir*
seen	*sá, séð, sén*
sending-men	*sendimenn*
sent	*sendi, sendir*
separate	*skiljast*
set	*sett, setti, settur, setur*
shall	*skal*
shared	*deili*
sharply	*snarpir*
she	*hana, henni, hér, hún*
sheathed-sword	*skeið*
she-wolf's-head	*ylgjarhöfuð*
shield	*skildi*
shield-maiden	*skjaldmær*
shield-maidens	*skjaldmeyja, skjaldmeyjar*
shimmering	*skjóma*
ship	*barð*
ship-fleet	*skipaflota, skipaflotann*
ships	*skip*
ship's-course	*skipaferðum*
ship-steering-man	*skipstjórnarmaður*
shoe-thong	*skóþvenginn, skóþvengur*
short	*skjóta*
shortage	*skorta, skorti*
shorter	*skemur, skjótara*
should	*mun, muni, skildi, skuluð, skyldi, skyldu*

Word List (English to Old Icelandic)

English	*Old Icelandic*	English	*Old Icelandic*
show	*lýsa*	start	*hefjast*
sickness	*sótt, sóttin*	statements	*ráð*
side	*megin*	steered	*stýrði*
sides	*megin*	stem	*stofni*
sister	*systir*	stepped	*sté*
sit	*sitja*	stewards	*sýslumenn*
skills	*list*	stiff-footed	*stirður*
slayings	*vígaferði*	stood	*staddur, staðið, stóð, stóðu*
sleep	*svefni*	storm	*hríðmál*
slept	*sofnaði, sofnar*	straight	*drjúgt*
small-stones	*smágrjót*	straightaway	*þegar*
so	*sá, sem, sjá, slíku, sú, svo*	strain	*hneig*
so-as	*að*	strength	*afli, magni*
soft-bed-prepared	*umbúnaður*	stricken-sun	*hnigsólar*
sold	*seldur*	striking	*hjuggu*
some	*sumir*	striking-distance	*höggfæri*
someone	*nokkur*	strong	*sterkur*
something	*nokkuð, nokkur*	struck	*höggur*
some-time	*eitthvert, nokkuð*	subduing	*brýtur*
somewhat	*nokkuð, nokkur, nokkurs*	subjects	*þegnum*
son	*son, sonar*	such	*slíka, slíks, slíku, slíkum, svo*
son-of-Helgi (name)	*helgason*	such-like	*þvílíks*
Son-of-Hrodbjart (name)	*roðbjartssonr*	summoned	*kvatt*
soon	*brátt, snemma*	supervision	*umsjá*
soonest	*skjótast*	swooping	*svipan*
sorcery	*fjölkynngi*	sword	*hjörs, sverði, sverðinu*
sought	*leit, leitaðist, sækja*	swords	*sverða*
sound	*sundunum*		
speak	*talar*		
spear	*skafti*		
spear-guardian	*geirvaldr*		
spears	*geiri, vigrum*		
speech	*máli*		
spite	*böls*		
spoke	*kvað, kvaðst, mælt, mælti, mæltu*		
spoken	*mælt*		
stain	*áta*		
standing	*staddir, standa*		
star	*stjörnu*		
Star-Oddi (name)	*stjörnu-odda, stjörnu-oddi*		
stars	*stjörnur*		

T, t

English	*Old Icelandic*
take	*taka, takast*
taken	*taka, tekinn*
takes	*tekst*
tall	*hátt*
teeth	*tönnum*
telling	*sagði, sögu*
temple	*hofs*
Temple-Head (place)	*höfða, hofshöfði*
tens	*tugum*
test	*reyna*
than	*en, í*
thanked	*þakkaði, þakkar*

Word List (English to Old Icelandic)

English	Old Icelandic	English	Old Icelandic
that	á, að, en, enn, er, hinn, hvað, sá, sem, það, þann, þar, þeirri, þetta, til	the-king	konung, konungi, konunginn, konunginum, konungr, konungs, konungsins, konungur, konungurinn, siklingi, siklingr
the	á, að, en, er, hið, hin, hina, hinn, hinni, hins, hinum, í, það, þau, þess, þessi, þetta		
the-assembly	þing	the-kingdom	ríki, ríkið, ríkinu, ríkis
the-battle	bardaga, bardaginn, orustunni	the-king's	konungs, konungsins, konungurinn, siklings
the-berserkers	berserkjanna, berserkjunum	the-king's-men	konungsmönnum
		the-king's-poet	konungsskáld
the-best	best	the-king's-ship	konungsskipið, konungsskipinu
the-blow	höggið		
the-bodies	hold	the-king's-sister	konungssystir
the-border	mörkinni	the-land	landi, landinu, lands, lönd
the-brothers	bræðir		
the-day	daginn	the-lands	lands
the-dream	draum, drauminn, drauminum	the-land's-people	landsfólkið
		them	þeim, þeir, þeirra
the-earl	jarl, jarli, jarls	the-matter	máli
the-earl's-daughter	jarlsdóttir	the-men	ljónar
the-evil-doers	illvirkjanna, illvirkjarnir	the-most	mest
the-feast	veisluna, veislunni	the-mound	hauginn, hauginum
the-fight	sameignar	themselves	sér, sig
the-firth	firrðist	then	á, að, en, hina, síðan, þá, það, þaðan, þann, þar, því
the-forest	skóginn		
the-goddesses	ásynju		
the-gods	véar	the-news	tíðindi
the-government	landstjórnin	the-night	nóttina
the-greatest	mestur	the-other	annar
the-guest	gesturinn	the-others	hinum
the-hand	handa	the-outlaw-men	útilegumannanna
the-helm	hjálmi	the-people	alþýða, mönnum
the-helmsman	hilmis	the-poem	kvæði, kvæðið, kvæðinu
the-highway	þjóðbrautinni		
the-hill	hólinn, hólinum	the-poet	skáld, skáldi, skáldinu, skálds
the-house	húsinu		
their	sín, sinna, sitt, þeirra	the-queen	drottning, drottningar, drottningin
theirs	sínum, þeira, þeirra	there	þangað, þar, þau, þeir, þeiri, þeirra
the-island	eyjarinnar		
the-journey	ferð, ferðinni	therefore	því
the-key	grafinn	the-ring	hringinn
		the-robbers	stigamönnunum
		the-robbing-men	stigamannanna

Word List (English to Old Icelandic)

English	Old Icelandic	English	Old Icelandic
the-saga	sagan, sagði, söguna, sögunnar, sögunni	throw	skjóta
		thrown	varp
the-sake-of	sakir	tied	bindur
the-same	sæma, saman	time	tíma, tímar
these	þenna, þessa, þessar, þessi, þessir	times	sinni
		t-look	sjást
the-sea	sjár	to	á, að, af, en, í, svo, það, til, vit
the-ship	skipan, skipi		
the-ships	skipanna, skips	to-be	verða
the-sound	sundin, sundunum	to-do	gera
the-stars	stjörnum	together	saman, samför
the-surf	lágarða	togetherness	samför
the-tables	borðum	to-have	láta
the-toast	erfinu	to-hear	áheyrsla
the-treasure	féið	to-her	henni
the-treasurer	gunndjarfr	to-him	hann, honum
the-truth	satt	to-know	vita
the-way	gata	told	getið, sagðag, sagði, sagt, talað, töldu
the-weather	veðri		
the-wedding	brúðhlaup	told-of	getið
the-wicked	svikmenni	to-me	mér
the-woman	kvenna	to-meet	hitt
they	það, þær, þar, þau, þegar, þeim, þeir, þeirra	too	of
		took	leiðir, næmdu, nam, takast, tekur, tók, tókust
they-are	eru		
they-were	voru	toothed	tindótt
things	hluta, hluti, hlutum	to-other	öðrum
think	hugsað, hygg	to-travel	fara
thinking	hugur	toughness	harðfengi
thirty	þrítug	to-you	þér, yður
this	sú, það, þenna, þess, þessa, þessar, þessarar, þessari, þessi, þessu, þessum, þetta	traditions	sið
		travel	færi, far, fara, farandi, farar, fari, ferðina, fóru
this-king	konungurinn	travelled	fara, fer, fór, fórst, fóru
thong	þvenginn		
Thord (name)	Þórður	travelling	farið, ferðina
though	þó, þótt, þóttist	travel-weary	farmóður
thought	hug, hugði, hugðu, mundi, þætti, þótt, þótti, þóttist, þóttust, þyki	treasure	fé, fyrðar
		treasured	dýrmörum
		trees	börva, viður
		trollish	tröllslegt
three	þrjú	trolls	trölls
throne	stól	trust	treysta
		truthful	sannsögull
through	úr	turned	snýr

Word List (English to Old Icelandic)

English	Old Icelandic
twelve	*tólf*
two	*tveggja, tveir, tvo*

U, u

English	Old Icelandic
un-alert	*ósnöfurmannlega*
un-courteous	*ólát*
under	*und, undan, undir*
unequal	*ójafnað, ójafnari*
unfolded	*rekka*
unheard-of	*endemi*
uninvited	*óboðið*
unlocked	*luku*
un-pleasant	*ódælli*
un-swinging	*ósvífr*
until	*uns*
unusual	*fáheyrður*
up	*upp*
upon	*á*
upright	*rekkum*
urged	*fýstu*
us	*oss*

V, v

English	Old Icelandic
valiant	*böðfrækn*
various	*ýmissa*
verse	*vísur*
verses	*vísur*
very	*einkar*
victory	*sigri, sigur*
victory-gift-gods	*sigrgöfgaðir*
viking	*víking*
viking-raids	*víking*
vikings	*víkinga, víkingar*
virtuous	*dyggir*
vision	*fyrirburður, víst*
visions	*fyrirburð*
visit	*vitja*
voyage	*ferðar*

W, w

English	Old Icelandic
wafting	*hvofta*
wake	*vakni*
wall	*vegg*
wanted-to	*vill*
war-clothes	*herklæðum*
war-company	*herliði*
warfare	*herför, vígroða*
warrior	*gramr*
warriors	*drengir, gramr, grams*
was	*enn, er, eru, sem, væri, var, varð, vera, voru*
was-heard	*spyrjast*
was-named	*hét*
waves	*bylgjur*
way	*leið, veg, venja*
ways	*vega*
wealth	*fé, fjár, fjárins*
wealthy-treasures	*auðæfum*
weaponed	*vopnaðir*
weapon-nimble	*vopnfimi*
weapons	*vopnum*
weapons-exchange	*vopnaskipti*
weight	*vægis*
well	*allvel, vel*
went	*færu, fór, för, fóru, gekk, gengu, gengur*
were	*er, væri, var, voru*
we-sailed	*sigldum*
what	*en, er, hvað, hverra*
when	*er*
where	*er, hvar*
which	*en, er, sem*
while	*hríð, meðan*
who	*er, hver*
whole	*heilum*
wide	*breiðan, víða*
widely	*víða*
wield	*valda*
wife	*eiginkonu, kona, konu*
wife-of	*kona*
will	*vil, vill*
willed	*vildi, vildu, vilja*
willing	*fúsastur*
will-you	*viltu*
windswept	*byrsóta*

Word List (English to Old Icelandic)

English	Old Icelandic
winters	*vetra*
wise	*fróður, vitrustum, vitur*
wisest	*vitrasta*
wish	*vil, vilji, viljið, vill*
wished	*vildi, vildu*
with	*að, enda, með, of, úr, við, víða*
within	*innan*
without	*utan*
woke	*vaknaði*
woken	*vaknað*
wolf	*heiðingja*
wolf's	*ylgjar*
woman	*kona, kvenna*
women	*konur*
won	*gagn*
wonder	*undrast, undur*
wonderful	*ágætum*
wonder-like	*undarlegt, undarlegur*
wood	*skíð, víði*
worded	*orð, ort*
words	*málma, orð, orða*
word-struggle	*orðahjaldur*
working-man	*verkmaður*
worth	*verður, virðing*
worthily	*virðulega*
worthiness	*virðing, virðingu*
worthy	*verða, virðing, virðulegri, virðulegur*
would	*mundi, mundu, muni*
would-be	*væri*
wounds	*sárum*
written	*ritnar*

Y, y

English	Old Icelandic
yet	*þó*
you	*þér, þig, þú, yður*
young	*ung, unga, ungur*
your	*yðvarrar, yðvarri*
yours	*þín*
yourself	*sjálfum*
youth	*æsku*

A Word Comparison of Old Norse and Old Icelandic Words

Old Norse	Old Icelandic	English	Old Norse	Old Icelandic	English
áðr	áður	after	biðr	biður	invited
áðr	áður	before	bindr	bindur	tied
ærit	ærið	abundance	blíðliga	blíðlega	joyfully
ætlat	ætlað	intend	boðit	boðið	invited
aftr	aftur	back	borit	borið	bore
aftr	aftur	returning	borit	borið	brought
ákafliga	ákaflega	extremely	borit	borið	carried
aldri	aldrei	never	brattr	brattur	broad
aldrigi	aldregi	never	Bregðr	bregður	reaction
aldrs	aldurs	of-age	brýtr	brýtur	subduing
allbráðliga	allóráðlega	all-un-forethought	búit	búið	preparations
			búit	búið	prepared
allráðligt	allráðlegt	advisable	bundit	bundið	bound
alþýðu	alþýða	the-people	Dagfinnr	dagfinnur	Dagfinn (name)
alvápnuðu	alvopnuðu	all-weaponed			
andaðr	andaður	died	dreymði	dreymdi	dreamed
Annarr	annar	one	dróttning	drottning	the-queen
annarr	annar	the-other	dróttningar	drottningar	queen
annat	annað	another	dróttningar	drottningar	the-queen
Annat	annað	one	dróttningin	drottningin	the-queen
annathvárt	annaðhvort	another-either	drukkit	drukkið	drank
annathvárt	annaðhvort	either-way	drukkit	drukkið	drunk
at	að	a	dýrðlig	dýrðleg	glorious
at	að	in	dyrigætti	dyragætti	doorway
at	að	it	eðr	eða	or
at	að	of	eiskranlig	eiskranleg	rage
at	að	so-as	ek	eg	I
at	að	that	ellifu	ellefu	eleven
at	að	the	elligar	ellegar	otherwise
at	að	then	erendi	erindi	errand
at	að	to	fá	fái	get
at	að	with	færi	færu	went
atburðr	atburður	events	fáheyrðr	fáheyrður	unusual
atburðr	atburður	happening	fara	fari	travel
aufúsa	öfúsa	gratitude	farit	farið	gone
austr	austur	east	farit	farið	travelling
bar	þar	there	farmóðr	farmóður	travel-weary
betr	betur	better	fátkaðist	fáttkaðist	few
bezt	best	best	feðr	föður	father
beztu	bestu	best	fegrst	fegurst	fairest
beztum	bestum	best	féit	féið	the-treasure

A Word Comparison of Old Norse and Old Icelandic

Old Norse	Old Icelandic	English
fekk	fékk	got
fell	féll	fell
fellu	féllu	fell
fengit	fengið	got
ferr	fer	it-went
ferr	fer	travelled
firrðisk	firrðist	the-firth
flokkr	flokkur	flokk
forkunnliga	forkunnlega	exceedingly
frægr	frægur	famous
frændr	frændur	kinsmen
fremð	fremd	honour
fróðr	fróður	wise
fúsastr	fúsastur	willing
fylgð	fylgd	follow
fylldir	fylltir	filled
fyrða	fyrðar	treasure
fyrirburðr	fyrirburður	vision
Garpr	garpur	Garp (name)
gauzkrar	gauskrar	of-the-Goths
Geirviðr	geirviður	Geirvid (name)
gengit	gengið	gone
gengr	gengur	went
gerðisk	gerðist	came
gersamliga	gersamlega	completely
gerzt	gerst	done
gestrinn	gesturinn	the-guest
getit	getið	told
getit	getið	told-of
geysimikit	geysimikið	exceedingly-great
glaðliga	glaðlega	gladly
glöggliga	glögglega	clearly
göfugligum	göfuglegum	noble-like
gótt	gott	good
hægliga	hæglega	comfortable
hættliga	hættlega	dangerously
hæverskliga	hæversklega	modestly
haf	hafa	had
hafiðr	hafiður	raised
haukstóls	haukastóls	hawk-seat
heðan	héðan	from-here
hefr	hefir	had
heitit	heitið	dominion
heldi	héldi	held
heldr	heldur	rather
helt	hélt	held
helzt	helst	rather
herða	harða	hard
heygðr	heygður	buried
hezt	best	the-best
hezta	besta	best
heztum	bestum	best
Hildiguðr	hildigunnur	Hildigunn (name)
hingat	hingað	here
hirðmaðr	hirðmaður	court-man
Hjörguðr	hjörgunnur	Hjorgunn (name)
Hjörvarðr	hjörvarður	Hjorvard (name)
Hléguðr	hlégunnur	Hlegunn (name)
höfðingliga	höfðinglega	nobly
höfuðit	höfuðið	head
höggit	höggið	the-blow
höggr	höggur	struck
hógligr	hóglegur	comfortably
hon	hún	her
hon	hún	it
hon	hún	she
Hróðbjartr	hróðbjartur	Hrodbjart (name)
hugr	hugur	thinking
Hugsat	hugsað	think
huldu	huldu	covering
hváfta	hvofta	wafting
hvárir	hvorir	each
hvárki	hvorki	neither
hvárt	hvort	each
hvárt	hvort	either
hvárt	hvort	how
hvártveggja	hvortveggja	each-way
hvat	hvað	that
hvat	hvað	what
hvé	hve	how
hverr	hver	each
hverr	hver	who
in	hin	the
ina	hina	the
inn	hinn	the

A Word Comparison of Old Norse and Old Icelandic

Old Norse	Old Icelandic	English
inni	hinni	the
ins	hins	the
inum	hinum	the
inum	hinum	the-others
it	hið	the
Jöruskógr	jöruskógur	Battle-forest (place)
kallaðr	kallaður	called
kemr	kemur	came
koma	komi	come
komit	komið	came
komit	komið	come
kómu	komu	came
konungr	konungur	king
konungr	konungur	the-king
konungrinn	konungurinn	the-king
konungrinn	konungurinn	the-king's
konungrinn	konungurinn	this-king
konungsskipit	konungsskipið	the-king's-ship
köru	kjöru	chose
kostat	kostað	earned
kostr	kostur	choice
kostrinn	kosturinn	choice
kostrinn	kosturinn	distinguished
kunna	kunni	know
kurteisliga	kurteislega	courtly
kvæða	kvæði	announced
kvæðit	kvæðið	the-poem
kvánfang	kvonfang	a-match
kvánfangs	kvonfangs	a-match
kvánföngin	kvonföngin	a-match
kvángaðr	kvongaður	married
kveðit	kveðið	recited
kveðskaprinn	kveðskapurinn	poetry-making
kveldit	kveldið	evening
lagit	lagið	granted
landit	landið	land
landsfólkit	landsfólkið	the-land's-people
landsstjórnin	landstjórnin	the-government
lengr	lengur	longer
liðit	liðið	passed
líkligt	líklegt	likely
ljósliga	ljóslega	lightly
lokit	lokið	concluded
lokit	lokið	ended
lykðum	lyktum	completion
maðr	maður	a-man
maðr	maður	man
mætti	mættu	may
mála	málma	words
mannaðr	mannaður	brought-up
mannfallit	mannfallið	people-felling
Margt	mart	many
merkiligsti	merkilegasti	remarkable
mestr	mestur	the-greatest
mik	mig	me
mik	mig	myself
mikit	mikið	great
mikit	mikið	greatly
mikit	mikið	much
mjök	mjög	most
mjök	mjög	much
mjök	mjög	much
morgininn	morguninn	morning
munda	mundi	would
nætr	nætur	night
náliga	nálega	almost
náliga	nálega	closely
náliga	nálega	nearly
nát	náð	protection
nefndr	nefndur	named
nökkur	nokkur	something
nökkur	nokkur	somewhat
nökkurr	nokkur	someone
nökkurs	nokkurs	somewhat
nökkut	nokkuð	something
nökkut	nokkuð	some-time
nökkut	nokkuð	somewhat
norðr	norður	in-the-north
óboðit	óboðið	uninvited
of	um	about
óhægendi	óhægindi	inconvenience
ok	og	also
ok	og	and
ok	og	of
ök	og	and

A Word Comparison of Old Norse and Old Icelandic

Old Norse	Old Icelandic	English
ór	úr	from
ór	úr	out-of
ór	úr	through
ór	úr	with
orðahjaldr	orðahjaldur	word-struggle
orrostu	orustu	battle
orrostunni	orustunni	the-battle
örvígr	ósvífr	un-swinging
ósnöfrmannliga	ósnöfurmannlega	un-alert
prúðligsta	prúðlegsta	most-prolific
ráðligt	ráðlegt	advice
ráðvandr	ráðvandur	honest
reiknaðr	reiknaður	counted
ríkit	ríkið	the-kingdom
rjóðr	rjóður	clearing
sá	sáu	saw
sæi	sæju	saw
sæmð	sæmd	honour
sæmði	sæmdi	honour
sæmiligar	sæmilegar	honourable
safnat	safnað	gathered
sagðak	sagðag	told
sák	sá	saw
sé	séu	are
seldr	seldur	sold
sér	sért	are
sét	séð	seen
setr	setur	set
settr	settur	sat
settr	settur	set
sigr	sigur	victory
sik	sig	herself
sik	sig	himself
sik	sig	his
sik	sig	themselves
sjá	sjái	see
sjálfr	sjálfur	himself
skemr	skemur	shorter
skilði	skildi	should
skilðu	skildu	knew
skilnaðr	skilnaður	parting
skipstjórnarmaðr	skipstjórnarmaður	ship-steering-man
skor	skör	across
skópvengr	skópvengur	shoe-thong
skyldi	skyldu	should
sómasamligri	sómasamlegri	respectable
sonr	son	son
staddr	staddur	placed
staddr	staddur	stood
staðit	staðið	placed
staðit	staðið	stood
sterkr	sterkur	strong
stigamönnum	stigamönnunum	the-robbers
stígr	stígur	climbed
stirðr	stirður	stiff-footed
stofnat	stofnað	planned
stórmannliga	stórmannlega	great-man-like
svá	svo	so
svá	svo	such
svá	svo	to
svát	svo	so
Svipun	svipan	swooping
talat	talað	told
talði	taldi	said
tekr	tekur	took
þangat	þangað	from-there
þangat	þangað	there
þat	það	it
þat	það	that
Þat	það	the
Þat	það	then
Þat	það	they
þat	það	this
þat	það	to
þeira	þeirra	of-them
þeira	þeirra	their
þeira	þeirra	theirs
þeira	þeirra	them
þeira	þeirra	there
þeira	þeirra	they
þeiri	þeirri	that
þik	þig	you
þingat	þingað	assembled
Þórðr	Þórður	Thord (name)
þvít	því	because
þykki	þyki	thought
þykkir	þykir	seemed
þykkir	þykir	seems

A Word Comparison of Old Norse and Old Icelandic

Old Norse	Old Icelandic	English	Old Norse	Old Icelandic	English
þykkja	þykja	regarded	vegligasta	veglegasta	greatest
þykkja	þykja	seem	veittr	veittur	given
tíðenda	tíðinda	news	veizla	veisla	feast
tíðendi	tíðindi	news	veizlu	veislu	feast
tíðendi	tíðindi	the-news	veizluna	veisluna	feast
tíðendin	tíðindin	news	veizluna	veisluna	the-feast
tíðendum	tíðindum	news	veizlunni	veislunni	the-feast
tíginna	tiginna	high-born	verðr	verður	became
tígn	tign	prestige	verðr	verður	worth
tígnar	tignar	princely	verit	verið	been
tízka	tíska	fashion	verkmaðr	verkmaður	working-man
tját	tjáð	expressed	við	viður	trees
tölðu	töldu	told	vildi	vildu	willed
tröllsligt	tröllslegt	trollish	vili	vilji	wish
tryggðarmaðr	tryggðarmaður	faithful-man	vilið	viljið	wish
			villtu	viltu	will-you
tvá	tvo	two	virðuliga	virðulega	worthily
umbúnaðr	umbúnaður	soft-bed-prepared	virðuligr	virðulegur	worthy
			virðuligri	virðulegri	worthy
undarligr	undarlegur	extraordinary	virkðamönnum	virktamönnum	chosen-man
undarligr	undarlegur	wonder-like			
undarligt	undarlegt	wonder-like	virkðavinum	virktavinum	friends
undr	undur	wonder	viss	vís	aware
ungr	ungur	young	vissir	vísir	know
unz	uns	ours	vitr	vitur	wise
unz	uns	until	yðr	yður	of-you
útan	utan	without	yðr	yður	to-you
vá	vó	guarded	yðr	yður	you
vaknat	vaknað	woken			
ván	von	expected			
ván	von	expecting			
vanr	vanur	accustomed			
vápnaðir	vopnaðir	weaponed			
vápnaskipti	vopnaskipti	weapons-exchange			
vápnfimi	vopnfimi	weapon-nimble			
vápnum	vopnum	weapons			
var	varð	was			
vár	vor	our			
várr	vor	our			
várrar	vorrar	aware			
Váru	voru	they-were			
váru	voru	was			
váru	voru	were			
vaxit	vaxið	grown			